At the risk of over-simplificauon, ...
Moeller's message this way: Don't give up. Don't give up. I like
that message, because it is the profound message that has
brought Bill and me to the eve of our twentieth wedding
anniversary. We have had to work hard to build our life together
and at various times along the way we both felt like giving up.
Why didn't we? Because we were convinced that God had the
power to lead us through the tough times of marriage and into
joy-filled, mutually satisfying intimacy. Moeller believes that too,
and offers practical, biblical guidelines to help couples stay
together and allow God to accomplish His purposes in their
marriage.

> **Lynne Hybels,** author with husband, Bill Hybels, of
> *Fit to be Tied*

For Better, For Worse, For Keeps is a book that invites you to discover power and hope in the vows you made to each other. It
will challenge, encourage, and motivate you to love your spouse
in a transformational way. This book could be a turning point in
your marriage.

> **Dr. Robert E. Coleman,** director, School of World Mission
> and Evangelism, Trinity Evangelical Divinity School;
> director, Institute of Evangelism, Billy Graham Center

Bob Moeller understands the chemistry of marriage. He blends
those ingredients with his own exceptional storytelling abilities to
make this a book that will warm (or re-warm) your marriage and
minimize the chances of an explosion.

> **Marshall Shelley,** editor, *Leadership*

Whether you are contemplating wedlock or have been married
for a brief or a long time, this book contains the wisdom that
will produce intimacy and deep romance in your relationship.
Almighty God is honored and revealed in Bob Moeller's excellent
work.

> **Bill McCartney,** Promise Keepers

In a day when divorce has become the accepted solution to an unhappy marriage, Bob Moeller takes us back to the basics. He reminds us that when one's marriage faces tough times, the right question to ask is not, "How can I change partners, so as to *find* the right one?" Rather, it is "By God's grace, how can I so change as to *become* the right one?"

Through relevant illustrations from his own counseling experiences and knowledge carefully researched in the field, and by using the Scriptures (especially the unusual story of Jacob, Leah and Rachel) in a very effective way, he calls us to the marital "road less traveled"—self-sacrifice, character growth, and above all, commitment.

I plan to use this book as I counsel troubled spouses who need this reminder.

David A. Seamands, author of *Healing for Damaged Emotions*

This excellent book openly discusses some of the real and unpleasant conflicts that every marriage has to face. How these problems are resolved is the key to failure or success in marital relationships. Bob Moeller has some excellent suggestions that could enrich every marriage.

Beverly LaHaye, president, Concerned Women for America

Renewing your marriage in the tough times

FOR BETTER FOR WORSE
For Keeps

BOB MOELLER

MULTNOMAH BOOKS

FOR BETTER, FOR WORSE, FOR KEEPS
Renewing Your Marriage in the Tough Times

published by Multnomah books
a part of the Questar publishing family

© 1993 by Robert Moeller

International Standard Book Number: 0-88070-624-4

Printed in the United States of America

Scripture quotations are from the *New International Version*
© 1973, 1984 by International Bible Society
used by permission of Zondervan Publishing House

Moeller, Bob
 For better, for worse, for keeps: renewing your marrige in the tough
times/Bob Moeller.
          p. cm.   Includes bibliographical references.
ISBN 0-88070-624-4: $8.99
1. Marriage--Religious aspects--Christianity. I. Title.
BV835.M64 1994   93-2781
248.8'44--dc20   CIP

97 98 99 00 01 — 10 9 8 7 6 5 4

To my wife, Cheryl,
whom I love with all my heart.
To our four children,
who mean more to us than life itself.
And to our parents,
who taught us a lesson beyond value—
never give up.

Contents

Foreword

Not long ago, I found myself in the midst of a career change. After years of teaching, I became editor of a new Christian counseling magazine and, before long, publishers started sending us books for review. I wasn't surprised to find that many of these books dealt with marriage and family issues—issues like divorce prevention, divorce recovery, coping with abuse, building a better sex life, and guidelines for better parenting. Many of these books are repetitious, poorly written, not very helpful, and often a restatement of the obvious. But mixed with the mediocre, we find occasional gems that are refreshing, clearly written, practical, interesting, and fun to read. *For Better, For Worse, For Keeps* is one of these gems.

I first met the author when we worked at the same divinity school, but we really got to know each other when we began worshiping together. It didn't take long for me to discover that Bob Moeller is a gifted speaker, a devoted husband, a committed family man, and a warm and personable friend. He is specially gifted as a writer who brings a rich background to this book. As a former pastor, editor, and counselor, Bob writes with a freshness and a reality that surely will captivate readers.

When I was asked to write a foreword, I agreed to skim the manuscript but ended up reading the whole thing. I found myself engrossed in the writing of a man who draws from his counseling experiences, humorously shares his own foibles, gives a variety of case histories, and points us to biblical illustrations of marriages that faced tough times. This book is interesting, well written, useful, and filled with practical benefits for anyone who is contemplating marriage or is trying to keep a marriage alive and renewed during tough times.

Books on marriage are likely to keep rolling from the presses, largely because couples have so many stresses and because even good marriages are hard to keep alive and growing. In the midst of this flood of books, I hope that many people will reach for the volume you now hold in your hands. Even more, I hope that many will read it. If my experience is any indication, others also will find it entertaining, thought-provoking, and genuinely helpful. This is one book I am happy to recommend.

Dr. Gary R. Collins

Preface

I wish one book could cover all the vital areas of distress and problems that can occur in a marriage, but it's simply not possible. *For Better, for Worse, for Keeps* deals with the more common and negotiable problems in marriage. I urge those with more complex marital problems (particularly those individuals whose spouses are chemically dependent, unfaithful, emotionally or physically abusive, or who evidence disruptive emotional, spiritual, or psychological problems) to seek competent professional help immediately.

Let me also say a word about the illustrations and stories in this book. They are based on actual situations, or the composite of several individuals and situations. No story or illustration is unique to one person or couple. In each case I have seen more than one example of the type of problem or situation I describe in order to include it in the book. The names, locations, and circumstances have been significantly altered to protect identities. The problems and difficulties of marriage are so common and universal that some similarities to our own experiences are bound to occur. Solomon was right when he observed, "There is nothing new under the sun."

Finally, it's important to remember the purpose of this book is to offer couples hope, not guaranteed solutions. Ultimately, it's up to us as husbands and wives to seek out the answers we need, to invest the necessary time and energy to solve issues, and to commit ourselves to the hard work and sacrifices required to build a lasting and loving relationship.

That is both the difficult calling and the magnificent adventure of marriage.

Acknowledgments

Books just don't happen. That much I've learned during the last sixteen months. They're the result of the support, encouragement, and confidence of so many individuals. Family, friends, and colleagues have been an invaluable source of resolve and refreshment during this process. I shall never forget, nor be able to adequately thank, those people God used in our lives to help us finish this course.

I owe thanks to several people in particular. First and foremost to my wife, Cheryl, who brought her good judgment and perceptive insights to the venture, to my parents, Homer and Inez Moeller, who offered us their continual encouragement, and to our many friends who have stood with us through this long effort.

To Rod Morris, who was the first to take an interest in the idea, to Carol Bartley, a patient and insightful editor who did so much to bring it into its final form, and to Dan Rich, Rebecca Price, Shari MacDonald, Michele Tennesen, and Blake Weber, who each added their wisdom and creativity to the project. To all these people I offer my real and heartfelt thanks.

Finally, my gratitude to Don Jacobson and all the partners at Multnomah, whose vision to strengthen marriages and bring hope to families ultimately made the book a reality.

Chapter One

IS LOVE ONLY FOR THE LUCKY OR THE STRONG?

Martin and Helen have been married nearly forty years. To outsiders, their marriage would appear to be a success, but not everything is as appearances suggest. Early in their marriage Martin wanted to go overseas and teach English in a two-thirds world country. Helen resisted the idea, citing health concerns, poor pay, and the lack of good schools for the children. To accommodate his wife, Martin reluctantly gave up his dream and has spent his career in a civil service position instead.

Today he finds himself struggling with anger and resentment toward her. He seems obsessed with the past, imagining what life could have been like if he had not listened to her. "If only," he says day after day to himself. "If only I had followed my heart."

Phil and Cynthia have been married just seven years. Phil comes home from work one day and finds the house strangely quiet. When he walks up to their bedroom, he discovers Cynthia's closet is empty. Bewilderment soon gives way to panic, and Phil begins furiously searching the house for some clue to what has happened. In his hunt, he at first misses the obvious—a note pinned to a throw pillow on the bed. Trembling, he picks it up and scans its contents.

"Dear Phil, this is the hardest thing I've ever done in my entire life. But it's the only way I know to get your attention. I've been trying to tell you for a long time that I couldn't go on with things the way they are. But you wouldn't listen. Maybe now you will. Don't try to contact me. Right now I just need space. Love, Cynthia."

No one sees Phil for two days. He doesn't even call in sick at work. He just sits in the living room by himself, unable to react.

Jim and Janene are on the third day of their honeymoon in the Caribbean. Seated on the balcony of their hotel room overlooking the crystal green ocean and coral white beaches, Janene believes it is the ideal setting for love. But Jim is unusually quiet.

"What's wrong, dear?" she asks, reaching out for his hand.

Jim feigns a smile. "Nothing, sweetheart."

"No, really, something's bothering you. Please tell me what it is."

Jim looks away, a pained expression on his face. He is silent for a long while and then turns toward his new bride. "Janene, I've been struggling the last few days."

"With what?"

"I'm not sure…" he hesitates, trying to decide if he should say what is on his heart. Finally he takes the plunge. "I…I'm not sure if I should have married you. I don't know if I love you or not."

Janene stares at her new husband for a moment, trying to absorb the shock of what she has just heard. Then, without a word, she gets up from the table and runs inside. Even though she closes the door behind her, Jim can hear the muffled sobs coming from the bathroom. He feels awful, awful for what he has just said, awful because it's true. But with this difficult confession he has experienced a certain relief. At last his agony is no longer a secret.

FROM PASSION TO PAIN

What do these three stories have in common? They're stories of marriages that have gone from "the better" to "the worse." They're examples of people who need to learn to love each other again and to discover that God's plan for their lives includes the person they married "for keeps."

Many people believe that lifetime love is only for the lucky or the strong. It's not. God's design for marriage is for every couple to know true intimacy, deep fulfillment, and the exhilarating experience of being loved just for who they are.

Yet, the design for marriage and the reality of marriage often don't match. Each year millions of couples choose divorce, adultery, or an armed truce as a means of coping with a disappointing marriage. But it doesn't have to be that way.

For Better, For Worse, For Keeps is a book about hope—hope for couples who have watched their marriages go from a passionate love affair to a daily annoyance, or even worse. But it isn't a book just for marriages on the brink. It is for any couple who desires to renew their love and commitment to their marriage. Hope, love, grace, a fresh start, a second chance—these are the essential elements of renewing a marriage when the going gets tough.

An experience I had in high school might serve as a useful analogy. I was earning extra money at the time by working nights as a janitor in the Department of Agriculture building. Besides cleaning bathrooms and emptying wastebaskets, I was assigned a highly critical task: buffing the tile floors on the perimeter of the office complex.

You may not be familiar with what a buffing machine looks like. It resembles an upright vacuum cleaner with handlebars and a giant circular disk on the bottom the size of a manhole cover. As the disk spins around at the speed of light, it polishes the floor.

Using only one finger, the foreman demonstrated the relative ease of operating this high-powered machine. He slid the machine effortlessly back and forth across the tile. Together, he and the buffing machine resembled an Olympic figure skating pair, gliding on ice, responding in perfect synchronization to each other's moves.

"There they go, Janet. This is the last move in the compulsories. They're going to attempt a double axle. Yes! They've done it! A perfect 10!"

"Do you think you can handle it?" the foreman asked.

"Piece of cake," I replied.

"Good. I have to leave early tonight, so it's your job to do the entire floor by nine o'clock."

As the foreman waved good night, I swaggered up to the machine like John Wayne approaching his horse. I grabbed both handles, closed my eyes, and squeezed the trigger. The machine bolted away from me like a crazed Doberman pinscher on a short leash.

I desperately tried to hang on as the machine careened from one side of the hallway to the other. It would bang into one wall and then dart off for the other side. As the night wore on, I was repeatedly punched in the stomach by the handlebars, thrown into the wall by the centrifugal force of the disk, and dragged down the hallway. I consoled myself with the Russian proverb, "Every beginning is hard." In this case it was brutal.

As the clock approached nine, I was frantic to finish. I came to the section of hallway outside the head supervisor's office (the Grand Poobah of the Agriculture Department). By now I had managed to gain some control over the buffing machine, and my internal injuries weren't life-threatening. Taking the machine firmly by the handlebars, I determined I would emerge the victor over the buffer or die trying. Steeling myself for the attack, I grabbed it with both hands and hit the switch. This time the machine glided quietly across the floor like a cowed puppy.

"That's more like it. Now we see who's boss," I smirked.

But the machine had only been toying with me to lull me into a trap. As soon as we reached the doorway of the supervisor's office, it leaped from the floor onto his carpet (a move it had been planning all along). I stood helpless, unable to react as the buffing machine whirred round and round, driving all the dirt, wax, and foreign particles from the hallway deep into the plush pile of the chief executive's carpet. I may be the only custodian in the history of the Department of Agriculture to have buffed the boss's rug. Stunned by this surprise attack, I retreated from the office before I could do any further damage, dragging the machine with me.

The next day I came to work prepared to pick up my last paycheck. As I approached the foreman, a grin crept across his face. "I see you had a little problem last night."

"I guess it got away from me," I mumbled.

"Don't worry. I cleaned it up before work this morning. The supervisor doesn't know anything about it. You'll get the hang of it."

GRACE: DON'T LEAVE HOME WITHOUT IT

For reasons I still don't understand I was given a second chance when I really didn't deserve one. That's the nature of grace.

You may have been pummeled, punched, and dragged down the hallway by the disappointments in your marriage. The fabric of your relationship may be marred by deep, ugly, and stubborn memories. You may be all but certain it's over. That's where the power and strength of your vows can carry you through the tough times you're facing. You can learn to love again.

Your promises to each other can put your marriage back on track. But to turn "for worse" into "for better" you will need to give and receive grace from one another. You will need to put the past behind and allow love to be rekindled. You will need to go beyond disappointment and despair and seek the beauty and reality of true intimacy. Fortunately, God is in the business of grace and will help you each step of the way.

A friend of mine was going through a difficult phase in his marriage when he came home one day to find the oak coatrack standing in the middle of the hallway. His wife had covered it with yellow ribbons and placed on it a note that read, "Who cares if it's not a real oak tree. Any old oak tree will do. I love you." His encounter with her unconditional love was a breakthrough. From that day on, their marriage started to change, for better.

In preparation for this book, I spent considerable time researching the popular advice on marriage given in our culture. Some advice I found helpful, some questionable, and some downright absurd. However, the more serious research done on marital relationships confirms one important fact: A person's best hope for experiencing happiness and fulfillment in marriage is to stay with the same partner for a lifetime.[1] Which leads me to agree with Ralph Waldo Emerson, who observed, "The only way out is through." There is no simple way out of the difficulties and tough times you may be facing at the moment. But there is a way through, a way that leads to greater happiness and contentment. Helping couples find that way through is the purpose of this book.

May God be with you as you seek that higher route.

Chapter Two

CHECKING IN AT HEARTBREAK HOTEL:

Where Did Our Marriage Go Wrong?

Susan was a sweet, rather ordinary looking young woman who had never had a steady boyfriend until she met Scott. She wasn't all that attracted to him but was flattered by his romantic attention. If nothing else, his companionship kept her from sitting home alone on Saturday nights.

As time went on, Scott's interest in Susan became more serious. When he finally proposed, she wasn't sure what to do. Although they had been dating for quite a while, Scott was hardly the man of her dreams. He had a dependent personality and was a chronic complainer. Still, Scott was a man, and this might be her only opportunity to get married. So against her better judgment, she said yes.

Did she really love him? That thought troubled her as she picked out china, drew up the guest lists, and asked friends to serve as bridesmaids. I can learn to love him after we're married, she would tell herself. After all, I won't have any choice then.

When Susan's doubts about Scott would return, she would think back to the difficult days in high school and college when the phone was silent, weekends were long and lonely, and prom nights came and went without her. She never wanted to be that alone again.

Susan successfully managed to keep her anxieties in check until the day of her wedding. Standing at the rear of the church, adorned in white, holding a beautiful bouquet in her hands, she looked down the aisle—and froze. It was as if her subconscious pulled off the gag she had been using to silence it for so long.

What am I doing here? she thought to herself. I don't love Scott. I'm not even sure I like him. Seeing him standing at the front of the church suddenly made her feel sick. No rationalization would silence her fears now. Why am I going through with this? her mind screamed.

Desperate, she began glancing at the doors, the exit signs, the stairwells—anywhere that might provide an escape from the building. But then another thought seized her. What would my parents think? What would the guests say if I refused to go through with this? Imagine the embarrassment if I ran out of the church. Her heart was pounding, and her thoughts were racing out of control. Was it all a bad dream?

As the music began to swell and the crowd rose to its feet, she was overwhelmed by the two hundred faces looking her way. They were waiting for her, smiling and nodding. Could she disappoint them? Her family? Scott?

It's too late; I can't back out now, she thought to herself. I have to go through with this. I'll work out my doubts about Scott later. Right now, I have to do what everyone's expecting me to do.

Closing her eyes, with her legs threatening to buckle underneath her, she started down the aisle. Feeling as if she was somehow outside her body and simply a spectator to this event, she arrived at the altar, took Scott's hand, and completed the ceremony. It was, in her own words, the worst decision of her life.

Today Susan is troubled, if not obsessed, with the desire to live her life over again. She longs for a chance to turn the clock back just this once. This time she would not marry Scott. This time she'd have the inner strength to leave the church. This time she'd marry someone handsome, sensitive, and romantic. If life would give her just one more chance, she wouldn't make the same mistake twice.

But the clock cannot be turned back. Her wedding day cannot be relived. Because her religious convictions won't allow her to divorce Scott, she's resigned herself to living the rest of her life with a decision she regrets making. She feels trapped.

JACOB AND LEAH'S STORY: IT CAN'T GET WORSE THAN THIS

Susan and Scott are not the first two people on earth to wake up after the wedding and find themselves in a difficult and painful marriage. Unfortunately that same story, with variations in details, happens over and over again every day. In fact, painful as your marriage might be today, I doubt it could be worse than the story of Jacob and Leah, two people who never had any intention of getting married, but who ended up as husband and wife. Their story offers fascinating insights into the dynamics of a marriage all wrong from day one.

Jacob was born into a family of destiny. His father, Isaac, was the only son of Abraham, the great patriarch of the nation of Israel. God had promised Abraham that all the earth would be blessed through his descendants.

But by rights Jacob's older twin brother, Esau, was set to inherit the family blessing and birthright. Jacob, however, through a series of cunning moves, stole Esau's birthright and the blessing of his father, Isaac.

When Esau realized he had been deceived out of his inheritance by Jacob, he vowed blood revenge. Forced to flee for his life, Jacob ran into the desert in search of a sanctuary. It could have been the end of Jacob, but God had mercy on the young man. Nearly exhausted by heat and thirst, he happened upon a fresh well owned by a shepherd named Laban, who turned out to be his uncle, the brother of his mother Rebekah. Even more remarkable, Laban had a daughter of ravishing beauty—Rachel.

It looked like Jacob's fortunes were changing. In the desert he had found family and a woman who had captured his heart. But Jacob's deceptive lifestyle was about to catch up with him.

What Goes Around, Comes Around

When Jacob asked for Rachel's hand in marriage, Laban rubbed his chin and thought for a moment. "I'll tell you what," he said. "Stay and work for me for seven years, and in return I'll give you my daughter's hand."

"Fair enough," Jacob at last responded, casting a glance at the lovely Rachel. The two men shook on it, and for the next seven years Jacob divided his time between grazing sheep and gazing at his fiancée.

Was Jacob anxious to get married? Listen to what happened when the seven years ended.

Jacob said to Laban, "Give me my wife. My time is completed, and I want to lie with her."

So Laban brought together all the people of the place and gave a feast. But when evening came, he took his daughter Leah and gave her to Jacob, and Jacob lay with her. And Laban gave his servant girl Zilpah to his daughter as her maidservant.

When morning came, there was Leah! So Jacob said to Laban, "What is this you have done to me? I served you for Rachel, didn't I? Why have you deceived me?"

Laban replied, "It is not our custom here to give the younger daughter in marriage before the older one. Finish this daughter's bridal week; then we will give you the younger one also, in return for another seven years of work."[1]

Jacob couldn't believe it. He had been the victim of an elaborate "sting" operation. Just as Jacob had deceived his brother Esau and his father Isaac, now Laban had done a number on him.

For Jacob to have Rachel, whom he wanted desperately, he had no choice other than to accept his devious uncle's terms. But it would mean working seven more years and spending the rest of his life married also to Leah, a woman he had never had any romantic interest in. Reluctantly, Jacob said yes. The writer of Genesis captures the sad state of affairs between these unwilling partners in just two sentences: "[Jacob] loved Rachel more than Leah. And he worked for Laban another seven years."[2]

The Woman behind Curtain Number One

How could a story like this happen? How could anyone spend his wedding night with the wrong woman and not notice?

Two explanations have been offered. To begin with, it's possible Jacob had imbibed a bit too much of the fruit of the vine during the wedding festivities. By nightfall he may have been so drunk that he couldn't tell the difference between Leah and Rachel. However, the more likely explanation is that his wife had worn a veil, and it wasn't until the next morning he got a good look at who was behind curtain number one. Once he did, he knew with certainty he didn't like Laban's version of "Let's Make a Deal."

Not only did Jacob feel cheated, Leah was also a victim. What should have been a day of celebration turned out to be a day of bitterness. We can only imagine that while Jacob fumed and cursed his bad fortune, Leah wept and grieved over her cruel situation. Few things are more difficult to bear than the knowledge your marriage isn't working and the chances for true love have passed you by.

CHARACTERISTICS OF A MARRIAGE IN NAME ONLY

Although few modern marriages begin in such a bizarre fashion as Jacob and Leah's did, their story does offer us insights into the traits of marriages that have gone off the track. And when we know where a marriage got off track, we can find ways to restore it.

A Constant State of Misery

Jacob and Leah, though unhappily married, did not live entirely separate lives. They ended up having several children together. The customs of the day demanded that the husband spare his wife the disgrace of a barren womb. So in Jacob and Leah's case, sex was primarily for procreation, rather than as an expression of intimacy or love. To Jacob, fathering children was likely more an obligation than a desire to build a family together. The lack of love in their marriage is evident from the story of the birth of their first child.

Genesis tells us that "Leah became pregnant and gave birth to a son. She named him Reuben, for she said, 'It is because the Lord has seen my misery. Surely my husband will love me now.'"[3] Imagine, Leah named her first son after the word for misery. But ongoing misery is a common characteristic of struggling marriages. Often one spouse lives in perpetual regret for saying, "I do," while the other languishes from lack of love.

Ranelle believed she had married beneath her. She was an accountant in a large corporation; her husband Keith was a service sector employee. Even though she had pushed him into marrying her, she resented him from day one. She would walk ahead of him when entering a party. She would publicly scold him for little mistakes he made. She would demand that he "get with it" and find a better paying job. In short, she resented him. As much as he tried to live up to her expectations and improve himself, it didn't work.

Leah knew Jacob didn't love her. That was obvious from the first day of their marriage. She would see Jacob and her sister Rachel disappear into his tent for the night. Imagine the hurt as Jacob would speak tenderly to Rachel in front of the servants, but perhaps ignore or be irritated with Leah. Perhaps Jacob brought gifts for his beloved Rachel and pampered her with clothes, perfume, and spices, while Leah was given nothing but the necessities of life. Is it hard to imagine why she named her first child "misery"?

Using Children to Try to Save the Marriage

Leah said something significant when Reuben was born: "Surely my husband will love me now." It's typical for couples caught in a sinking marriage to try to remedy their relationship by having a child. One spouse thinks, If I produce something my mate loves and values, then perhaps he (or she) will love and value me as well.

Unfortunately, what often happens is that after the baby is born there are three miserable people in a family instead of just two. I've watched many unhappily married couples bring children into the world as a method of solving their marital problems—a solution that virtually never works. (That is, however, by no means a justification for abortion.)

Why doesn't having a baby bring a husband and wife together? First, the child represents the unloved mate. The features, hair color, and smile don't matter. That baby is half someone else, the someone the mate doesn't want to be married to. Fathers who aren't bonded to the mothers demonstrate a low investment in the nurture and care of their infants. They won't change diapers, they won't buy toys, they take very few pictures. Why? Because the child represents a relationship they don't value.

Another reason the baby-making solution doesn't work is the added stress it brings. To an already tense situation add a screaming infant who demands nonstop attention and brings on sleep deprivation. That's a lot for even happily married couples to cope with. I know. We had four children in six years. My wife and I would actually stare in envy at people in the grocery store who looked as if they had slept eight hours the night before.

Finally, bearing a child won't bring a couple together because a baby can't change the heart of another person. Sadly, the power of selfishness, anger, and revenge overrides even the instinctual love a parent should have for his own flesh and blood.

Leah was hoping that by producing a firstborn son, a highly coveted prize in the Near Eastern culture, Jacob's heart would soften toward her. It did not.

Public Ridicule and Contempt

Unhappy couples often act out their unhappiness in public. They don't care if other people know they aren't in love or can't even stand each other. They are often so caught up in their self-pity and anger that they lose all sense of discretion.

That was the case with Jacob and Leah. The account of the birth of their second son speaks for itself: "[Leah] conceived again, and when she had given birth to a son she said, 'Because the Lord heard that I am not loved, he gave me this one too.' So she named him Simeon," which probably means "one who hears."[4]

Word of Laban's deception to marry off Leah to Jacob had no doubt spread throughout the village. Leah believed that word of her loveless marriage had reached even heaven, and she was convinced that only the pity of God had allowed her to bear Simeon, her second child.

Can't you see Jacob in the marketplace, complaining to others about Laban's treachery and his homely wife? If Leah had hoped two sons would awaken love in Jacob, she soon found out otherwise.

Spouses who aren't bonded to their mates will often let others know just how miserable they are. Word spreads, and the unloving spouses may even hope that will cause their mates to make a decision they themselves don't want to make—a decision to end the marriage.

Distance and Detachment

Another characteristic of a marriage off track is aloofness and disinterest. Listen to the account of the birth of Leah's third son: "Again she conceived, and when she gave birth to a son she said, 'Now at last my husband will become attached to me, because I have borne him three sons.' So he was named Levi."[5] Scholars believe the name Levi sounds like the Hebrew word for "attached."

That's often what is lacking in a troubled marriage—a sense of mutual attachment. One or both spouses go through the motions of marriage, but their heads and hearts are elsewhere. They just aren't bonded to each other. Through emotional Morse code they send each other the message, "I may be married to you, but I'm not really bonded to you. There's a part of me I'll never let you have—my heart."

That was Chuck's perspective. He was an impulsive person who also tended to be egocentric. He probably married Tanya because she came from old money. Or because he was lonely. Or perhaps because he wanted someone to help him start his computer business. In any case, he quickly lost interest in her once they were married.

When he came home at night, he would just ignore her. Although Tanya was an intelligent, well-educated woman, Chuck saw her as his intellectual inferior. So he rarely talked to her, listened to her, or asked her advice. Before long he was spending time with others he considered more of his caliber.

Distance and detachment—clear signs of partners who believe they could have done better.

Tortured by the "If Onlys"

Some couples get caught in the syndrome of thinking, "If only I had it to do all over again," or "If only I had married another person," or "If only I had remained single longer."

Jane and Greg were both products of troubled homes. Their unmet needs drew them to each other, and throughout high school they were inseparable. They walked hand in hand everywhere, oblivious to others, always talking openly of their plans to marry. When they graduated from high school, they did marry, but the delayed fuses from their troubled families of origin were set to go off. After the birth of their first child, the detonation occurred.

As their relationship went from bad to worse, Jane began to think of the boys she could have dated. What if she had married one of them instead of Greg? All her unhappiness could have been avoided. Rather than focusing on her marriage as she needed to, she put more emotional distance between the two of them.

Couples caught in an unhappy marriage look for relief wherever they can find it. Retracing our life's steps and wishing we had made different choices may provide momentary distraction, but ultimately it does nothing to bring reconciliation. It's an exercise in futility. What is more useless than perpetual regret? It can't change the past, and it handicaps us from facing present realities with courage and wisdom.

I Married the Wrong Person

The final common symptom of a distressed marriage is the soul-chilling thought, "I married the wrong person." It's a tragedy beyond words when spouses wake up one morning and decide they are married to the wrong person. Like midmorning humidity in August, their marriage suffocates them. Now all they know is they want out. It doesn't matter how, they just want out.

Not only did that thought seize Jacob, it gripped one of the world's best-known couples. Half a billion people watched their wedding. Dignitaries from virtually every nation on earth attended the event. An elegant yacht with dozens of servants escorted them on their honeymoon voyage through the Mediterranean Sea. The marriage of Prince Charles and Diana Spencer was without question the most celebrated and publicized wedding of all time.

Today they live in separate castles. Their children divide the holidays between the two parents. The press runs frequent stories of their purported trysts with outsiders. What happened? How did the fairy tale marriage of the century turn into a fable of heartbreak, acrimony, and betrayal?

Gossip columnists and kiss-and-tell books will speculate on the answer to that question for years, possibly for generations. Whatever lurid or enticing inside information may come to light, the answer to the *why* behind Charles and Diana's breakup comes down to this: They both came to believe they married the wrong person.

THE ROOTS OF TROUBLED MARRIAGES

It's obvious how Jacob and Leah ended up in a marriage neither enjoyed. Their troubles could be traced to Laban's elaborate deception. But there are other, more common, roots that can produce a troubled family tree. Let's look at some of the reasons men and women say "I do," only to end up wishing they had said, "Forget it."

I've Lost the Feeling

Couples who marry strictly on the basis of their feelings often find their feelings betraying them. Desperate infatuation turns into deep-seated hostility. As the expression says, "Emotions have no intelligence." Physical passions aren't necessarily connected with our rational faculties. We can be completely mesmerized by people with whom we have absolutely nothing in common.

Certainly physical attraction is one element of the mystery of love between a man and a woman, but it is meant to be only a minor movement, not the basis for the entire symphony. As Proverbs so aptly observes, "Charm is deceptive, and beauty is fleeting."[6] That's why couples who marry simply out of physical attraction for one another are usually in for discord once the fascination and infatuation wear off.

Research has revealed that the hormones which produce the warm sensation of being "in love" eventually lose their potency. They wear out. So higher and higher levels of the same hormone are required to produce the same feelings of exhilaration.[7] The conclusion: It will take something other than high-voltage body chemistry to keep a couple together for a lifetime. The hormones that produce a "romantic high" just can't be sustained.

Although this false assumption that love is a rapid heartbeat and flushed face keeps soap operas, perfume companies, and country music in business, it can prove disastrous for marriages. But there is hope for that type of troubled marriage. It requires giving up the adolescent notion that love is the rush you feel when you see the other person. That rush eventually gives out, but that's where real love just begins.

Too Much, Too Soon

If hormones have no intelligence, they also have no virtue. That is, they can't be counted on to help us make the right moral choice of whom to marry.

Kristine and Greg met at the office. Kristine was tired of living alone and was looking for romance and companionship. Greg seemed to offer just what she wanted, but the price he was asking was quite high.

Kristine had been raised to believe that premarital sex was wrong. She had always planned to wait and save her virginity for her husband. But Greg, sensing she lacked a strong will, kept up the pressure. Eventually, he wore her down.

They later married, but their relationship was in trouble from day one. Kristine was angry at Greg for the pressure he had put on her to compromise. Greg felt guilty about what they had done and began showing less interest in her sexually.

Couples who are sexually active before the wedding day put obstacles in their path to happiness. Although proponents of premarital sex and cohabitation before marriage claim it improves marital adjustment, the facts don't support the idea. Couples living together before marriage divorce at a much higher rate than those who do not. Marital satisfaction is greater for those who wait than for those who don't.[8] For a variety of reasons, premarital sexual activity can come back to disrupt a marriage years after the wedding. The best chance for good sex after marriage is no sex before marriage.

Mr. Perfect and Miss Ideal No Longer Live Here

Couples in love commonly idealize their future partner. In their own minds they reshape the other person to fit their perception of the perfect husband or wife. They typically avoid uncomfortable truths about the other person. Why ruin a perfectly good fantasy with harsh realities?

I've counseled couples preparing for marriage who assured me they were perfect for each other. Sensing I have Mr. Perfect and Miss Ideal sitting in front of me, I often throw them a curve ball and ask, "Why don't you two tell me about the worst fight you've ever had?"

That usually leads to a moment or two of silence before one breaks the news to me. "Uh, Bob, we've never had a major fight." Pausing for a moment to glance lovingly in the intended's eyes, he or she finishes the thought by saying, "And we plan to never fight. We're in love." The other person usually nods and smiles dreamily as if to say, "That's right. If you were in love, you'd understand what we're talking about."

I don't enjoy bursting other people's bubbles, so I proceed gently. "Isn't there anything about the other person you find annoying?"

"Not really," they both giggle.

"Well, if you were to have a fight, what do you think it would be over?" I ask.

Again there is a long pause. "I can't think of anything, can you, baby?"

"No, baby, I can't either," the other one swoons.

Leaning forward, I say, "It sounds as if you two believe you are perfect for each other. Perhaps you are. But I can't marry you until I find out if you're capable of resolving conflict in your relationship. Let's put this wedding off until you've had your first big fight and we can discuss how you worked it out. Then I can help you determine if you are right for each other."

I've come close to needing the electric shock paddles. The look of incredulity from Mr. Perfect and Miss Ideal defies description.

I'm worried about couples who are so caught up in their idealized view of each other that they can't see whom they are actually marrying. When reality hits, it will hit hard.

What drives people to overlook the character flaws in another person? Often it comes from being raised in a troubled home. When addictions, compulsions, and abusive behavior become a way of life in a home, the children grow into adulthood with huge areas of unmet needs. Nature abhors a vacuum, and so people are driven to fill that void. They turn to romance and relationships to try to fill their need for love and acceptance. Because they so badly want to believe another person can solve all their interpersonal problems and give them the intimacy they crave, they refuse to see people as they really are. Chances are, they are in love with the idea of love, and they are setting themselves up for one of the rudest shocks of their life.

The In-Laws Treat You like Outlaws

Steve and Laurie were raised in different Protestant denominations. Though they shared a mutual Christian faith and had reached a common spiritual understanding, Steve's parents were rigidly committed to their church and warned him repeatedly of marrying someone outside the fold. They firmly believed that unless their grandchildren were raised in their own denomination they had no hope of salvation.

At first Steve's parents tolerated Laurie, hoping perhaps that she would join their church. As it became apparent Laurie and Steve had other plans, his parents became increasingly hostile.

The entire matter came to a head one day when Steve and Laurie were having lunch with his parents. After the table was cleared, they all agreed they should discuss wedding plans, but Steve's mother took charge of the conversation.

"Laurie," she said, clearing her throat, "we raised Steve to be a faithful member of our church. We understand you were raised to believe somewhat differently than he. We respect your right to believe whatever you wish, but I won't have my grandchildren being born into a mixed marriage."

Steve blanched. He had no idea his mother was going to do this. "But, Mom," he interrupted, "Laurie is a Christian."

"Don't interrupt me, son. I'm not finished."

Laurie's face mirrored her anguish. She instinctively knew what was coming next.

"Steve's father and I have had to make a difficult decision. If you two go ahead with this wedding and don't promise that you will raise the children in our denomination, we won't be attending the ceremony."

Turning toward Steve's mother, Laurie said, "Mrs. Branson, I couldn't care less if you set foot in the church on our wedding day. If you want to ruin the happiest day of our lives in the name of your religion, then go ahead and do so." Then she stood up, grabbed her purse, and ran out the door, tears streaming down her face.

Steve glared at his mother with a mixture of anger and disbelief, and then without saying a word he followed Laurie out the door. Looking out the window, Mrs. Branson could see the two of them sobbing and holding on to each other.

Problems with in-laws have led more than one couple to the brink of divorce. Sometimes the issues are as minor as giving unwanted "helpful hints" regarding housekeeping, finances, or child rearing. Other times they are more serious. Parents desperately cling to their son or daughter and refuse to give them up. They call constantly, demand attention, or find some way to keep their child committed to them first and foremost. If couples don't draw the proper boundaries with in-laws, the underlying tension and division that result can lead a couple to the point of dissolution.

I Already Hired the Organist

One of the worst reasons to marry is because we feel we owe it to the other person. But it happens every day. Marriage should be an act of love, based on a clear and reasoned choice, motivated by a desire to give, anchored in the firm and unshakable conviction this is the person we wish to spend the rest of our life with. It isn't an IOU to be paid out because our sexual behavior caught up with us or because we feel sorry for someone and want to rescue him or her. Nor should someone choose to go through with the ceremony simply to please others or to avoid embarrassment.

A popular woman's magazine carried the story of a young woman who got married despite her misgivings because it pleased so many other people. The title of the article, "I Knew My Marriage Was a Mistake—at the Reception," says it all.

Why we are willing to risk an entire lifetime of misery to secure the nodding approval of others is a mystery. But in many cases, engaged individuals feel that their fate is sealed and it's too late to back out. The tragic result is that although they go through with the wedding, they don't go through with the marriage. The young woman in this story divorced her husband less than eight months after getting married, but not before she cheated on him, humiliated him before his family, and left him brokenhearted and alone to sort out his life.

So Young, So in Love

Loretta Lynn, the famous country and western performer, was married while she was still a teenager. The story of her painful childhood union was chronicled in the movie *The Coal Miner's Daughter*. Her father's only admonition to her future husband was not to beat her, which he did anyway.

For many reasons, marrying too young often creates a distressed marriage. The most obvious is that few people are mature enough to handle the incredible demands and pressures of marriage when they're still essentially children. Life is nothing less than an extended struggle, and marriage adds to the complexities. It is no place for youngsters. The statistics tell us that teenagers who volunteer for duty more often than not end up casualties.[9]

Perhaps the most insidious aspect of marrying too early is the perpetual doubt it creates. Janice married when she was only eighteen. To this day she torments herself by asking, "I wonder if I would have married Jack if I had just waited another two years?" She has gone through her entire married life believing she was too young to know what she was doing.

I've met some happily married, well-adjusted couples who said "I do" long before they reached the age of twenty-one. They survived the rigors of battle and together became a cohesive team. It can be done. But statistics show it's the exception, not the rule.

Conclusion

Like Jacob and Leah, it's easy to wake up one day and ask, "I reserved the Honeymoon Suite, so how did I end up in Heartbreak Hotel?" When disappointments, problems, and despair enter the picture, it's easy to start looking for a way out, any way out. But rather than look for a way to escape, which can create more problems than it solves, it is better to understand what brought you to this point and what can be done to get back on track. As we'll learn later in the lives of Jacob and Leah, the early chapters of a painful marriage are not the entire book.

Chapter Three

SEARCHING FOR THE
ESCAPE CLAUSE

A pril fifteenth is a day few Americans celebrate, unless of course they have decided not to pay income taxes. That's the case with a Chicago man who claims he's found a loophole in the Sixteenth Amendment to the Constitution, the act which authorizes Congress to impose federal income taxes. He's so sure he's right that he hasn't given Uncle Sam a dime since 1976.

He has published an extensive two-volume work that documents alleged irregularities in the way states ratified the amendment nine decades ago. According to him, he's under no obligation to pay the federal government anything because the law is null and void.

Uncle Sam has responded by indicting him for tax evasion. It remains to be seen if a jury will believe he has the right to thumb his nose at the law because of a loophole he claims to have discovered. Should he win his case, the government would probably owe the rest of us about ten trillion dollars in illegally gathered back taxes. But should the jury find him guilty, he'll be given time to research further his novel theory while experiencing the comfort of all-expenses-paid living quarters, food service, and twenty-four-hour security, courtesy of the federal government.

It's human nature to seek exemption from the rules. People who find themselves in unhappy or unfulfilling marriages often try the same thing. When the marriage goes bad, they start scanning the fine print of their wedding contract to find a quick and painless way out. But it doesn't exist, and attempting to walk out on their responsibilities eventually lands them in a prison of their own making.

What are the more popular "escape clauses" people use to get out of the promises they made on their wedding day? Foremost is divorce.

THE BIG "D"

In the space of fifteen years, from 1965 to 1980, the divorce rate more than doubled in the United States. Not coincidentally, in the early 1970s states began passing "no-fault" divorce laws. Essentially these laws removed the burden of having to provide a compelling reason to dissolve the marriage contract. Fault no longer had to be proven, so if someone wanted out of a marriage, he or she could get out, no questions asked.

The Rockford Institute, a think tank located in the Midwest, has documented that divorce rates rose dramatically in states that adopted "no-fault" laws. Rather than solving the problem of divorce in our society, the laws threw gasoline on the fire. Common sense would have predicted the accelerated breakup of marriages. The easier it becomes to break a promise, the more often it will be broken. In the last three decades, families began to come apart.[1]

The very notion of "no-fault divorce" was ridiculous to begin with. No-fault divorce makes as much sense as no-fault adultery, no-fault theft, or no-fault slander. We can change the semantics as often as we wish, but divorce is still an unnatural and painful injustice inflicted on another person (even if both people agree to it). It is breaking promises, and no-fault promise breaking is simply not possible.

The people of ancient times, eager to find the fine print in their marriage vows, once asked Jesus, "Is it lawful for a man to divorce his wife for any and every reason?"

Jesus chose not to deal with technicalities but pointed to the grand purpose and design of marriage. "'Haven't you read,' he replied, 'that at the beginning the Creator "made them male and female," and said, "For this reason a man will leave his father and mother and be united to his wife, and the two will become one flesh"? So they are no longer two, but one. Therefore what God has joined together, let man not separate.'"[2] What was he saying about marriage and divorce? It's intended "for keeps."

Can you rip a seamless garment in two without doing permanent damage? Can you hammer a priceless sculpture and maintain its beauty? Can you saw a living organism in two without inflicting enormous pain and suffering? That's why God considers divorce immoral; it destroys in a painful and unnatural manner a special work of his creation intended to last a lifetime. To suggest we humans can do just that for "any" and "every" reason is to devalue what God himself prizes so highly.

That's why claiming that no one should bear any fault for willfully destroying such a precious relationship is close to preposterous. How can we destroy the emotional security of another human being, wipe our hands, and announce, "It isn't my fault"? How can we tear in two the hearts of children by forcing them to choose which parent they will live with and then say, "So what? It's best for everyone involved"? How can we break the most sacred of human vows and say, "Who cares? It was all a mistake"?

Yes, But Does It Work?

Let's put aside for the moment the question of whether divorce is moral and approach it from a purely pragmatic viewpoint. Does it accomplish what it's supposed to? Does it bring long-lasting relief from the pain, anxiety, and disappointment that come with an unhappy marriage? Does if offer a new lease on life, giving us the opportunity for a fresh start unhindered by the past?

Richard bought the line that divorce could solve his problems. His smallest mistakes, like spilling coffee or forgetting to pay a bill, would send his wife into a tirade. When Richard finally grew tired of her temper and nagging, he decided divorce was the ticket out. He could unload his wife and go shopping for someone who would treat him with more respect.

Right after the divorce was granted, Richard felt relieved. It was like walking out of prison into the sunshine. Now he could go on with his life. Soon, however, he began wrestling with deep bouts of loneliness and sadness. The reality of severing the most intimate bond in his life wasn't as painless and easy as he had imagined.

In an effort to fill that void, he began dating again. Eventually he met Denise. She had recently divorced as well, and both agreed their first spouses had been first-class losers. Their romance took off like a greyhound on a racetrack, and almost immediately they were talking about marriage. When they tied the knot, they believed this was the beginning of a new chapter in their lives.

Before long Richard made a startling discovery. Denise, who had seemed mild-mannered and patient, was as capable of violent mood swings as his first wife. She was a perfectionist, tormented by anger and a sense of inferiority, and so Richard again found himself on the receiving end of someone else's rage. He was stunned to realize he had gone through the pain of a divorce only to end up in an identical situation. How could it happen to him twice?

The answer is quite simple. Richard expected more from divorce than it can deliver. It can change our partners, but it can't change who we are. Richard had assumed the problems in his life were caused exclusively by his spouse. All he had to do was get rid of her, and his problems would exit with her.

Albert Ellis, the distinguished psychologist, developed a list of irrational beliefs that guide the lives of many people. One such belief is that "happiness is dependent upon external circumstances or other people." Richard had fallen for that misconception. He believed divorce would change his external world and clear the way for him to be happy.

Does divorce work? From my observation, and from the testimony of numerous divorced individuals I've worked with, the answer is no. It trades one set of problems for another, with the second set often being far worse.[3]

Is It Better for the Kids?

Parents who are feeling guilty about breaking up their home often rationalize that "it's better for the children this way." They reason that an unhappy marriage, filled with angry glares, slamming doors, and silent meals, is far worse on children than no marriage at all.

Newsweek devoted a major article to this topic in January of 1992. The article begins with the story of Sara Dadisman: "It was her thirteenth birthday. Even now, two decades later, talking about it is difficult for her. 'It seems as though my mom did it to almost hurt me,' says Dadisman.... 'Sometimes I think, Was that real? Did she really do that on my birthday? But I can remember her giving me a present, a Barbie doll or something, and then telling me she and my dad were getting a divorce. I was devastated.'"[4]

Several years ago I was moved as I watched a movie about a boy who hires a lawyer to stop his parents from divorcing. The boy claims he is "a necessary party" to the marriage contract and, as such, should be consulted before a divorce is granted. His sister, so traumatized by her parents' separation, begins wearing earmuffs in the middle of summer to keep from hearing any more painful news.

When the case is finally heard in court, the boy argues successfully that there is no compelling reason for his parents' marriage to end. Listening to their son's pleas, the parents are moved to reconsider their decision to destroy their home and their children's happiness.

The final scene of the movie shows the boy and his sister walking down a sidewalk together.

"Do we still have a family?" she asks.

"We still have a family," he replies.

Rigging the Jury against Future Happiness

Claire Bergman, author of *Adult Children of Divorce Speak Out*, says poignantly, "A hole in the heart is universal. There is a sense of having missed out on something as a birthright, the right to grow up in a house with two parents."[5]

I have many friends who were utterly devastated by their parents' divorce. Even after they were grown and married, most never fully recovered from the shock. A sense of invalidation lingers. It's as if they say, "The very union that brought me into existence is broken."

Not only does divorce leave children with track marks across their heart, it rigs the jury against their having a successful marriage later in life. *Newsweek* discovered this significant trend:

> Compared with people who have grown up in intact families, adult children of divorce are more likely to have troubled relationships and broken marriages. A desire for stability sends them down the aisle at too young an age, and they wind up in divorce court not long afterward. Others fear commitment because they learned too well the lessons of their childhood—don't trust anyone, not even Mom or Dad. Even when divorce releases children from their parents' violent or emotionally abusive marriage, they worry that they don't know how to be half of a happy couple because they've never see one close up at home.[6]

Despite a thousand and one reasons to end a marriage, the emotional need of children to have two parents refutes them all. You may find a different husband or wife, but your kids will never find another mother or father. Parents who truly love their children will give them the gift that only they can offer—a stable and loving marriage. That's why kids will blush and turn away when they see their parents kiss. They're embarrassed with delight. Each display of affection ties one more rope of security around their heart.

Popular magazines suggest that after decades of a social experiment in human tragedy, even the so-called experts are rethinking their attitude toward divorce. If the cure doesn't work and causes more pain and suffering than the disease, perhaps it's time to switch treatments.

GIVING A TRYST A TRY

The second most common escape clause that unhappy and unfulfilled spouses try is the affair. It seems to offer the best of both worlds. You can keep your current husband or wife and yet enjoy the thrill of a new love. You can get the wild, unrestrained passion of a honeymoon without the hassle of clogged sinks, measles, or afternoon carpools. It seems to offer the "for better" without the "for worse."

To be honest, few people sit down and say to themselves, "I think I'll break my wedding vows and have sex with a person I'm not married to." Affairs usually begin much more subtly. People find themselves with unresolved emotional pain or unmet needs. Their spouse is either unaware of what's going on or is unconcerned. Over time, the hunger for intimacy—although initially not in a sexual sense—begins to grow.

Then comes the opportunity. Someone at work, or next door, or even at church begins to show common courtesy and respect. This person is also feeling unfulfilled, and the illusion of intimacy draws the two together.

David Seamands, a well-known marriage counselor and author, tells about counseling a woman caught up in an affair she wanted to end. To help her break the emotional tie to her illicit lover, Seamands told her to bring all the tokens of their relationship and throw them away. He had expected her to hand over a bottle of perfume, a love letter, or perhaps even jewelry. Instead, she produced a daily devotional book, *My Utmost for His Highest.* "Don't ask any questions," she said, dropping the book on his desk. If the marriage isn't meeting the spouses' spiritual, emotional, or physical needs, and they start scanning the horizon for a solution, they become prime candidates for adultery.

It can happen to almost anyone. The author of the majority of the book of Psalms was King David of Israel. He is described in the Bible as a man "after God's own heart." He was a courageous warrior, a powerful ruler, and a passionate poet. Yet the

Bible records that he committed adultery, had the woman's husband murdered, and then tried unsuccessfully to cover up the whole affair. He suffered the consequences of his foolish behavior for the rest of his life, as his children warred with one another and eventually tried to topple him from his throne. The decline of David's otherwise prosperous and successful life can be traced to the night he spent with Bathsheba.

Is an Affair Good for a Marriage?

Many in our society believe that an occasional fling with another person actually helps a marriage. Advocates of "open marriage" have suggested that couples be free to engage in sexual relationships with others as they choose. That takes the pressure off the mates to be the exclusive provider for their needs. Perhaps the high-water mark of such thinking was in the 1970s when people experimented with all sorts of relationships.

What's wrong with an occasional dalliance to enliven a boring and stale marriage? Isn't monogamy a quick ticket to monotony?

To begin with, sex is more than a biological act. It is the union of two people on a physical, emotional, and spiritual level. No human act involves the totality of a person like sexual intercourse. That's why it is to be reserved exclusively for our lifelong mate. The ancient book of Proverbs recognized this truth. "Drink water from your own cistern, running water from your own well. Should your springs overflow in the streets, your streams of water in the public squares? Let them be yours alone, never to be shared with strangers."[7]

The writer was saying nothing is more private, intimate, and exclusive than your sexual identity. Don't cheapen and denigrate who you are by sharing it "with strangers."

The results of a society that has chosen to ignore this advice are frightening. Josh McDowell, who has studied adolescent sexual behavior, recently stated there are now over fifty varieties of sexually transmitted diseases. That's an increase of several fold from just thirty years ago.

Health officials quietly acknowledge there is no "safe sex" outside of a lifetime monogamous relationship. Condoms have at best a 10 percent failure rate, and the HIV virus can potentially be spread simply through the perspiration present in the genital area during intercourse. In other words, if you want to place yourself in the lowest possible risk group for contracting the fatal disease, "Drink water from your own cistern, running water from your own well."

But it is not only the physical dangers adultery poses that should cause people to rethink their behavior. It is the personal, psychological, and relational damage that infidelity causes as well.

Can You Scoop Fire into Your Lap?

Adultery has a curious way of destroying everyone who gets involved in it. How many governors, public officials, and prime ministers have been brought down in shame when their private lives revealed moral compromise? How many pastors, evangelists, and media celebrities have been forced from the pulpit due to infidelity? How many millions of marriages have been irretrievably ruined because a man or woman broke the promise to "forsake all others"? Proverbs asks the question, "Can a man scoop fire into his lap without his clothes being burned? Can a man walk on hot coals without his feet being scorched? So is he who sleeps with another man's wife; no one who touches her will go unpunished."[8]

Sexual innocence is one item given in equal amounts to each man and woman. It can be preserved or squandered, but once it is lost, it is lost forever.

As appealing as adultery might seem to a person in a difficult marriage, it is the wrong choice. The only freedom it offers is the right to leave your integrity and reputation behind and to endure the disappointment and reproach of those who have trusted you the most. Solomon wrote, "A man who commits adultery lacks judgment; whoever does so destroys himself. Blows and disgrace are his lot, and his shame will never be wiped away."[9]

I watched the career of a minister go down in flames because of his tryst with a secretary. His church was devastated by the revelation. He repented and publicly acknowledged his sin. His wife stood by him. Then he fell again. And again. Finally, he was driven from the ministry permanently. His wife died prematurely. His daughter lost faith in life and God. Were the few minutes of excitement worth the price of a destroyed ministry, marriage, and child?

That's the reality of adultery. It isn't glamorous. It isn't fulfilling. It isn't a solution. Ask those who have had to live with the consequences of adultery, and if they're completely honest with you, most will admit it was the worst mistake of their lives.

It's said that when the smallpox virus reached the Hawaiian Islands it devastated the native population. It was a new disease against which the islanders had no natural immunities. While many died of the disease itself, many more needlessly died from pneumonia. When struck by the high fever smallpox generates, they rushed into the cool waters of the Pacific to find relief and contracted pneumonia. A serious problem turned into a fatal one through a remedy more dangerous than the disease.

The same is true of adultery. Rushing into an affair to find relief from an unhappy marriage is a dangerous decision. The headaches of marriage are mild compared to the consequences of sexual infidelity.

LIVING WITH AN "ARRANGEMENT"

As a new pastor several years ago, I decided to visit some of the elderly members of my congregation, including a couple in their late eighties who had been married well over fifty years. From the moment I stepped into the living room, I could have cut the tension with a knife. The couple seated themselves at ninety-degree angles to each other, and rather than talk directly to each other, they asked me to mediate.

"Pastor, tell her to stop nagging me about my chores," the old man said.

"You can tell him I'm not nagging him. He just won't admit that he needs to slow down. Tell him he's a stubborn mule," she countered.

And so it went. When I finally left the house, I was relieved that at least no toasters had been tossed my way. I couldn't believe it. After fifty years they still weren't speaking to each other.

For unhappy couples who reject the idea of divorce, and would never consider having an affair, the third option is usually what is called an "arrangement." They agree to stay together, but to live separate lives. They share the same roof, but seldom the same bed. They have their names on the mailbox, but rarely on anniversary cards to each other. To the outside world they look like a happy household, but inside, the four walls of their home are papered with animosity and resentment.

I once visited a couple in which the man was dying of cancer and had, at most, two months to live. Although he and his wife had always had a stormy marriage, I thought that perhaps now, as the end was so close, they would soften toward each other. But as I sat in the living room that day, trying to show concern and love for the dying man, she stormed in and berated him for forgetting to take his medicine. Their patterns were so deeply ingrained that they could not change, even in the face of death.

Living Alone Together

Few people stay in unhappy marriages anymore. In my parents' generation, couples would admit they made a mistake getting married, but they would often negotiate an armed truce. It didn't create loving marriages or stable home environments for children, but it kept them from experiencing all the problems of divorce or adultery. People would sleep in different parts of the house, eat alone, and often go to church by themselves.

Today I see the same phenomenon in marriages where husbands and wives essentially lead separate lives. They keep separate checkbooks, work different schedules, and take vacations by themselves. The spouses merely share expenses and household duties and occasionally appear with each other in public. The marriage is primarily a business partnership.

I believe many couples who settle for an arrangement once genuinely loved each other. They got married believing they would intimately share their lives and end up in their seventies or eighties walking down the street hand in hand. They never foresaw the day when their lovemaking would be as exciting as mowing the lawn or balancing the checkbook. They never dreamed they would go for an entire week without eating a single evening meal together. Nor did they anticipate it would be more fun to spend a weekend with friends from the office than with each other.

What happened? They starved their relationship to death. Strong marriages take time. Willard Harley, a marriage therapist and author of *His Needs, Her Needs*, claims that a couple needs fifteen hours a week of uninterrupted time alone to maintain a healthy marriage.

But when you subtract the time spent commuting to work,

putting in a full day at the office, working out at the health club, doing household chores, attending meetings, and catching up on reading or the latest movies, today's couples have precious little time left to work on intimacy and communication. They may have achieved their career goals, hopped onto the corporate fast track, and bought the largest house in their subdivision, but it was at the expense of the one relationship intended to last for a lifetime.

For example, couples who spend their leisure time in individual activities or with people other than their spouse are more likely to experience marital distress. You can't build a relationship if you aren't spending time together.[10]

Let me illustrate. I have always been an amateur gardening enthusiast (I need to stress the word "amateur"). When we moved to our new community, I read in the paper that the village gardening club rented plots in the summer to residents. I jumped to the phone, called the president of the organization, and learned there were just two plots left. "I want them both," I said proudly. Miracle Grow is about to find itself another world champion, I thought to myself. Even as I hung up, I imagined myself wheeling home bushels of plump tomatoes, ripe green peas, and succulent corn on the cob. Perhaps I would even have to cart my excess harvest to the local farmer's market on Thursday mornings.

When I went to inspect my two choice plots, I discovered they were so far at the other end of the field that the people rototilling their plots on the other side looked about three inches high. I also discovered my plots were an enormous distance from the nearest water spigot. I would need the hose from the local fire brigade to reach my garden. No problem, I thought, it's bound to rain a good deal this summer.

The day of our wedding anniversary I dragged Cheryl to a local nursery to buy an assortment of seedlings and plants to jump-start my garden. For the next two hours we lovingly planted tomatoes, green beans, bell peppers, lima beans, corn, and a variety of leafy vegetables. I assured Cheryl that our efforts would be rewarded by lowering our veggie budget that summer. When I finally put the last shoot in the ground, I announced we could then go out and have our anniversary supper together.

Every now and then I would drive by our plots and nod my head in satisfaction. Even though I couldn't see my garden from the road—at least not without binoculars—I knew in my heart that champion greens were bursting through the earth at that very moment.

Days passed, and I found myself preoccupied at work. My son was in baseball, my wife was exhausted from caring for our three preschoolers, and I was trying to sell a car. So most nights by the time I got home and finished supper and helped put the kids in bed, I was too tired to drive to the plots.

But the rains came that summer as I had hoped. In fact, it rained and rained and rained. After several weeks of neglecting the plots I took my children with me to check on them. We weren't in the garden for more than two minutes. Mosquitoes the size of pigeons came swarming out of the grass and trees and chased us back to our car.

Then it was time for our three-week vacation. By our return home in August, I hadn't been to the plots for over a month. I suddenly remembered the ominous memo the garden club president had issued at the beginning of the summer, "Individuals who do not tend to their garden will not be granted privileges for the next year." Fearful of the garden's condition by now, I did the only natural thing a person does when dreading the truth—I avoided it.

By the end of August I could no longer put off the inevitable. Taking a trusted friend with me for moral support, I drove to the garden. I knew it wouldn't be pretty, but a man has to do what a man has to do.

"Come with me. I'll show you my two plots," I said to my comrade. We walked forever past rows of huge watermelons, oversized squash, and towering corn. At last, we reached the stakes indicating my land.

"Where is it?" he asked innocently.

"Where's what?" I retorted.

"Your garden. Where is it? I don't see it anywhere."

I looked around. He was right. The garden had entirely disappeared underneath weeds as tall as mature oak trees. I got down on my knees and dug through the grass, looking for any sign of vegetable life. But the entire garden had just disappeared.

The weeks of neglect had taken their toll. My labor of love now looked more like a jungle than a vegetable plot. The closest I would come that summer to enjoying fresh vegetables was drinking a can of V-8 left in the bottom of the refrigerator.

Marriage is much like gardening. We can start off with high hopes and grandiose expectations, but as we are distracted by the pressures of daily living and the pursuit of other goals, the weeds begin to grow. Given time, they start to take over. Given enough time, they choke the life out of every healthy plant in the soil. Then comes the day, often too late, when we discover the enormity of our loss.

As I said earlier, I don't believe people set out to ruin their marriages. Few people return home from honeymooning in the Poconos or in Florida intent on ignoring their partner for the rest of their lives. Newlyweds opening gifts at the reception aren't thinking, Some day we'll show more courtesy to the UPS delivery man than to each other. But it happens.

Should you find your marriage in the same condition as my garden, do something. Don't let apathy and negligence choke out the last bit of life in your marriage. Don't settle for barren matrimony. Fight back. Regardless of how unfruitful the last several months or years have been, don't give in to the lie that love can't be renewed.

Rekindling the Flame

Within the character of God there is grace—the unearned, unmerited, freely given favor of God. When all seems hopeless and feelings of love toward our spouse are only a memory, the grace of God can do what we never thought possible. It can breathe life into a marriage that died years ago. It can restore tenderness to a relationship crusted over by years of apathy and neglect. It can revive a first love that has occupied last place in our life.

One of the most difficult interviews I ever conducted as a writer was with a couple who had absorbed several seismic shocks in their marriage. First, John and Nancy discovered their children had been molested by a teenager in their church. When they tried to expose the crime, the church refused to acknowledge it.

John's income wasn't meeting expenses, so he was forced to resign his job and look for work elsewhere. During this time, Nancy discovered she was pregnant—with twins. With little or no health insurance, they struggled to keep their heads above water financially. Soon after the birth of the twins, Nancy was diagnosed with cancer and underwent a hysterectomy.

Nancy and John just couldn't cope. The daily trauma cauterized their feelings. They went through the motions of marriage, but they became strangers to each other, bonded only by their mutual pain.

During this time John and Nancy moved and began seeing a counselor. Nancy happened on a book entitled *Rekindled* by Pat Williams, the former general manager of the Philadelphia 76er's basketball team. Williams wrote about his marriage, which had nearly suffocated under the enormous pressures of his job. But he wanted his wife's love back, and he decided to fight for it.

When John read *Rekindled*, a spark was ignited in his own life. Despite the tragedy and suffering they had experienced, he was determined to win back his wife's love.

"The turning point came when John wrote a song and gave it to me," Nancy remembers. "I realized he was hurting as much as I was and that he still did cherish me."[11]

Marriage was never intended to be an arrangement of business associates. Marriage is meant to excite, stimulate, nurture, challenge, and encourage us for a lifetime. God's purpose is for it to provide us with intimate companionship, fulfilling partnership, and satisfying relationship. While the fire might not remain at the same level for a lifetime, the spark between two spouses should never die. Listen to the writer of Proverbs: "May your fountain be blessed, and may you rejoice in the wife of your youth. A loving doe, a graceful deer—may her breasts satisfy you always, may you ever be captivated by her love."[12]

An "arrangement" might be one solution to a troubled marriage, but it is far from the best. Why settle for less than what God has planned for you?

COMMITMENT—THE RIGHT CHOICE

Divorce, adultery, and an arrangement—each offers temporary relief at best, and in the end each creates more problems and pain than it solves. There has to be a better way—and there is.

The only way out is through. We can't run from our problems. Believe me, if there were a better alternative available to couples than gutting out the problems of children, sex, financial pressures, in-laws, aging, taxes, and all the other tough issues in life, someone would have found it by now.

When my wife was expecting our first child, she suffered incredible nausea during that first trimester. If she even smelled coffee or bacon, she would double over right on the spot. I've never felt so helpless in my life. I went to the grocery store a dozen times, searching for something she could keep down—all in vain.

She continued to get worse, and finally the decision was made to hospitalize her. At the time we had no health insurance, and I was searching for a job. As her health deteriorated, there were days when I wondered if either she or the baby would survive this ordeal (or if I would).

"Just wait," the doctors would assure us. "This will probably pass when she reaches the second trimester." Terrific. That meant still more weeks of cleaning up vomit, going to the emergency room for intravenous feeding, and watching my wife suffer.

How many days we both wished there were an easy way out of the nightmare. One night she had a reaction to the anti-nausea drug prescribed for her, and the muscles in her neck tightened so that she was partially paralyzed. At that point I got angry. I stalked through the house moaning, "I've had enough of this. I can't take it any longer. I'm sick and tired of living this way." (Of course Cheryl was the one with the actual problem. I had just decided it was my turn to be seated at the head table of a pity party thrown in my honor.)

But we were committed. Committed to preserving the life of the baby, committed to the decision to become parents, and committed to seeing this thing through. Sure enough, just as the second trimester began, a remarkable thing happened. I was eating a sandwich one day when my wife looked over at me and said, "I think I'd like a bite of that." In utter disbelief I handed her the sandwich and watched her take a few, tentative bites. I was overwhelmed. At last, at long last, she was able to eat again.

Six months later our first child was born. "It's a boy!" I yelled in the delivery room. Tears came from pure joy.

Commitment, sheer commitment aided by the grace of God saw us through those agonizing days. And because we stuck with it, we have a son (and three other children) who are the supreme joys of our life.

When marriage partners think they can't take another day and they want an easy way out, my counsel is to remember "the only way out is through." There is no question about it—commitment is the only solid foundation for a marriage. The hurricanes of life may tear off the roof over your head, blow out the windows around you, and leave you knee-deep in water, but when the storm is over, your relationship will survive.

No Love without Risk

Few generations in the history of our nation have been more fearful of commitment than this one. William Willimon, a cultural observer, quotes the author of *The Postponed Generation*: "Committed, lasting relationships are a critical aspect of maturity. Today's young adults are having more trouble with relationships than with almost any other area of their lives." As Willimon points out: "Adolescence just goes on and on. Just 'living together' keeps commitment in limbo. Somehow, these 'special children' reason, there has to be a way to find love without risk. So a recent *New York Times* article speaks of this as 'The Uncommitted Generation,' where sex and love are merely an experience in 'Being Alone—Together.'"

That's an excellent description of our generation—"Alone—Together." People who want love without risk will never find it.

When Willimon was a part-time professor at Duke University, he once asked his students what they thought of the idea that living together outside of marriage is acceptable, as long as people are open, trusting, and caring. A young male student, barefooted and wearing a tank top and blue jeans, was the first to speak up. "I've lived through three or four of these so-called relationships. I'm here to tell you there's no way for them to be open, trusting, and caring, no way in heck without a promise. I hurt some good people to find that out. I wish the church had told me. I might still have learned the hard way, but I wish the church had told me."[13]

What the young man was saying is also confirmed by studies that document the negative impact of living together before marriage. Such couples report both a lower quality of marriage and a greater likelihood of divorce than those couples who did not cohabit before the wedding. In fact, the longer a couple has lived together, the more pronounced the adverse impact on their later marriage. If living together before marriage is supposed to strengthen a relationship, just the opposite happens.[14]

A *USA Today* headline once announced: "Warning: Life Can Kill You." That's just the point. All of life requires a certain amount of risk. We can't leave our house in the morning, pull onto the freeway, or sit down in the cafeteria for lunch without exposing ourselves to some risk. We can't even sit in our basement without the threat of radon gas seeping through a crack in the foundation. Life itself is lethal. There simply is no way to play it safe.

Who Needs a Marriage License?
Those who avoid marriage and opt for "no commitment" relationships run the greatest risks of getting hurt. They set

themselves up for a fall. Their unwillingness to commit virtually ensures they'll be taken advantage of.

Would we deposit our money in a bank that scorned deposit slips as worthless bits of paper? Would we buy a car from a dealer who scoffed at warrantees as outmoded and old-fashioned? Would we hand our credit card to a travel agent who thought issuing a receipt was for our parents' generation? We'd have to be crazy to do business with merchants who refused to make and honor a promise to their customers. Yet, when it comes to signing a wedding certificate or legalizing vows, the "no commitment" generation scoffs at marriage as archaic.

One of the saddest calls I have ever received was from a woman whose boyfriend just announced one morning he was leaving. "I can't handle our relationship any longer," he said. With that, he put his things in his car and drove off. The woman in tears asked if I could help bring him back. I was moved with pity and compassion, but there was nothing I could do. She had agreed to no commitment going into the relationship, and that's exactly what she got out of it.

There is absolutely no other foundation for happiness in human relationships than commitment. And that's part of growing up. As Willimon says so eloquently, "Welcome to reality. Life, you can be sure, has its grim side. Don't settle for anything less than a promise that will enable you to persevere in your love.…We Christians know of no happiness save that which arises as the by-product of commitment to another. We have no definition of love (a cross being on our altar) that is sacrifice- or risk-free. Relationships between men and women that go beyond merely hanging around take time, hard work, tough-mindedness, and a host of other virtues."[15]

Commitment begins with a promise. And if we keep our

vows, they'll keep us. One hundred couples married forty-five years or more were asked to tell what factors had contributed most to keeping them together in stable and satisfying marriages for over four decades. Their answers? Marrying someone you enjoy being with, keeping a sense of humor, agreeing on your life's goals, and not surprisingly—a commitment to each other and marriage.[16]

That's why of all the options available to couples struggling with their relationship, commitment is still the right choice.

Chapter Four

IF YOU KEEP YOUR VOWS, THEY'LL KEEP YOU

Over the years I have sat through some truly strange, if not bizarre, wedding ceremonies. I've heard excerpts from Barbra Streisand, *The Prophet*, and *Jonathan Livingston Seagull*. In place of lifelong, exclusive, binding commitments to each other, I have heard neutered, devalued, mass media "McVows":

> I, Diana, promise you, Lawrence, that I will always be there for you. I'll touch base often, and I'll do lunch with you when you're down and I'm not in Dallas. I will never encroach on your personal space, get dirt on your leather seat covers, or ask you to give up cross-training during the fall. I know that all these things so deeply define who you are as a person.
>
> In return, I ask that you honor my desire to drive a Lexus, to make fettuccine Alfredo for my mother, and to shop the outlet malls on Saturday. As Whitney Houston so beautifully sings, "One moment in time...." It is that moment I pledge to you.

As the bridesmaids (or bridesmen) dab tears from their eyes, deep calls unto deep, and the groom responds with an equally profound pledge:

> I, Lawrence, take you, Diana, to be my significant other. I will, from this day forward, give you full access to my CD library, my 486 SX personal computer with enhanced video graphics, and my Platinum Visa card. I'm offering you the chance to join me in a pursuit of our personal best, interfacing with one another in a network of our own, powering up together to face life. I shall never ask you to downsize your pursuit of excellence, give up trading in the commodity markets, or move your Nordic Track out of the bedroom.
>
> In return, I ask that you let our thoroughbred shelty sleep in our room, only buy romaine lettuce for our salads, and never allow fluorocarbons into the house. As my favorite performer, Billy Ray Cyrus, has so profoundly stated, "Please, don't break my achy-breaky heart." If you won't, I won't.

As easy-listening jazz plays in the background, the couple turns around and heads down the aisle to begin their newfound joint partnership, which has been spelled out and ratified in a ten-page prenuptial agreement (copies available at the back of the church). The lawyers shake hands in the reception line, and the deal is done.

FAST-FOOD VOWS

The only problem with these "McVows" is that they haven't promised anything resembling marriage. While they do touch on critical areas such as exercise regimens, stock portfolios, and ownership of sleek cars, they never mention the more upsetting and unpleasant topics such as sickness, poverty, and the most unmentionable of all—death.

Today, wedding vows are seen more as flexible goals rather than as solemn words of honor to be kept to the death. How else can you explain the staggering divorce statistics of the last two decades and the high percentage of men and women who admit to cheating on their mate? They've obviously been able to rationalize away the promises they made in front of God, the state, and their families.

And those people who are troubled by the idea of breaking a promise just don't make them, even when they get married. They rewrite the wedding ceremony and leave out the unpleasant parts—"for better or worse, richer or poorer, in sickness and in health." It's perhaps no coincidence that in the 1970s, the decade when divorce became all the rage, the popularity of writing your own wedding vows took off as well. If you didn't promise much, you hadn't broken much when you cut out.

ONLY A MATTER OF SEMANTICS?

Some have altered the traditional wording of the wedding vows to now read "for as long as we both shall love" instead of "for as long as we both shall live." The distinction between the two pledges is more than semantic; it's significant. The newer vows state that I'm only willing to stay married as long as I believe I'm in love. If I lose the feeling, if the tingle diminishes or the spark dies out, the relationship is toast. One bad fight, one lousy weekend, or too many visits from the in-laws, and it's time to start searching the yellow pages for an attorney.

Notice the subtlety of the new emphasis. My pledge isn't based on what I choose, but what I feel. So if I no longer feel like

I love my spouse, then I'm no longer obligated to keep my vows. I can cheat on my mate, trash my promises, and break up our home—all because my feelings have changed.

But if you read the traditional vows closely, you find they don't contain any escape clauses, except one—death. The only way a marriage was designed to end is at a funeral. That's the Creator's bottom line for commitment; it's for keeps.

The promises we made at our wedding ceremony are not only considered by the state to be a legally binding, enforceable, permanent contract, but by God as well. He designed the idea of marriage. Imagine getting your photos back and discovering God standing in the middle of the wedding party. I suspect that would cause all of us to hesitate more before reneging on our vows.

As our society has devalued the integrity and permanence of wedding vows, we have dramatically decreased the chances of finding lasting fulfillment in marriage. The easier it is to get out, the easier it becomes to give up. The result is a culture of desperately hurting, lonely, and unhappy people who trade in spouses the way they trade in used cars.

It's my conviction that a promise isn't a promise until we keep it even when we no longer want to.

My wife and I quickly discovered how difficult life can be and how vows will be tested, even when you are in love. While we were still engaged, we put our names on a waiting list for married student housing. But when we returned to school as newlyweds in the fall, there were still no openings. So we set out to find an apartment off-campus that could become our own little love nest. As newlyweds all we wanted was a place to snuggle and study until graduation.

All we could find was a converted garage. (I came later to question the sincerity of its conversion experience.) If I were to try to entitle our first year in this dwelling, I would call it "Dark Night of the Garage" (not to be confused with *Dark Night of the Soul*, a classic written during the Middle Ages).

When I say converted garage, I mean exactly that. The landlord had decided to boost his retirement income by refinishing the area and making it into an apartment. He did all the plumbing and electrical work himself, which became quite apparent once we moved in.

To begin with, every time the landlord's wife would do laundry and the washer would hit the rinse cycle, the brownish gray water would come gushing into our kitchen sink. We would have only ten seconds to run from the table and grab dishes from the sink before they were engulfed in swirling muddy water. If we listened closely for the sound of her washer, we could usually anticipate the deluge and save ourselves from having to scald the dishes. When we complained about this small inconvenience, she replied, "I don't see what you're so upset about. Our clothes aren't even dirty when we wash them."

Then winter arrived. And the cold winds began blowing. And the temperature dropped precipitously inside our apartment. For weeks we wore heavy sweaters, shivered under the covers day and night, and tried in vain to boost the temperature. The landlord and his wife were gone for several days—perhaps to a warmer climate—and could not be reached.

We were finally able to get one of their relatives to come and assess our situation. He poked around and eventually stuck his hand into the heating duct that went to the main furnace—and pulled out several inches of pink fiberglass insulation. For whatever reason, the entire duct had been stuffed closed with insulation, seriously impairing the flow of heat to our apartment. (If it was an energy saving device, it worked.)

We managed to hang on until spring when the rainy season arrived. Much to our surprise, we discovered we had rented lake-front property. Long before jacuzzis were in vogue, we had water lapping at our feet inside the living room.

A few weeks before our lease was up our landlord decided to throw a dinner party on the patio directly above our apartment. Call it coincidence, call it passive aggression, call it petty revenge, but I decided this would be a good night to cook out. I loaded our little grill with charcoal and then poured on enough lighter fluid to fuel a 747 aircraft on a transatlantic flight. When I lit the match, smoke billowed up, and a favorable wind wafted it across the patio. The singing and laughter from upstairs inexplicably came to a stop.

As you can imagine, all these adversities challenged our young marriage. I don't remember the specifics, but I think we did discuss once or twice whose idea it was to sign the lease. But the ironclad marriage vows we had exchanged the year before helped get us through our Dark Night of the Garage. We had promised both God and man we would hang in there, even when threatened by freezing temperatures, sinks full of back-wash, and floodwaters that reached our sofa. I'm glad we did.

Because we kept our vows, they kept us.

That's why I object so strongly to tinkering with marriage pledges. If we reword them to apply only as long as we feel love for the other person, a thousand and one things can happen to turn our dream house into a heartbreak hotel. It's when we're under incredible stress that genuine wedding vows show their true genius and power. They will get you through the worst possible moments of your life. They will bond you in a way that no cheap substitute can duplicate or imitate. As the commercial says, "Don't settle for anything less."

THE ONLY WAY OUT IS THROUGH

But if our marriage isn't working, and divorce, adultery, or an armed truce isn't the way to go, what should we do?

The way to renew a marriage doesn't begin with a change of emotions, but with an act of will. Renewal begins when we make the decisive choice to live up to the promises we have made. Even if we have broken them in the past, we can decide today never to do it again—and mean it. We can begin again where we first began—with vows that were meant "for keeps."

You may be thinking, "But, Bob, you don't understand. My marriage is so bad. It's so empty. It's so unfulfilling. Why in the world should I commit myself to staying in this dead-end relationship?" Because no problem can be solved by running from it. Remember, the only way out is through. I can't assure you that your marriage will be transformed overnight if you choose to keep your vows, but I can absolutely guarantee it will be ruined if you choose not to do so. The only hope toward restoring joy and fulfillment in our relationships is to live by the promises and pledges we made to our spouses. It's the design for marriage that works.

Perhaps the only thing going for your marriage at this point is the determination not to give up. After World War II the aging Winston Churchill returned to speak at the boarding school where he had grown up. The Lion of Britain had successfully led his countrymen through the worst experience in their modern history—the Battle of Britain. Bombs fell on London day and night for weeks on end with no relief from the outside world. Yet Churchill had stood firm and Hitler was turned back.

As the imposing Churchill struggled to get up from his seat, the room fell silent. Once he reached the podium, he studied the audience of fresh faces eager to hear what he had to say. He bellowed, "Never give up. Never give up. Never give up." With that, he sat down.

There is an enormous amount of truth in that short speech. The difference between the marriage that crashes and burns and the one that reaches the half-century mark is this: One couple gives up; the other does not.

Ultimately the only way to fail in life or in marriage is to give up. If we keep getting up, coming back, and refusing to say "die," eventually we will prevail.

MOVING FROM "I DO" TO "I WILL"

Glamour magazine published an article entitled "The Five Turning Points of Love." The author, Lesley Dormen, suggested that the most crucial decision of a love relationship is the last one, when a couple is ready to create something bigger than both of them. She illustrates with the example of Karen and Joe:

"On my wedding day, I remember looking at Joe in a kind of horror and thinking, Who is this stranger?" says thirty-two-year-old Karen. "I'd known all the guests for decades. I'd known the groom for only a year and a half!" Three years into the marriage, when Karen was pregnant, Joe's business failed. "Our commitment was really on the line. This wasn't, 'Will he remember our anniversary?' or 'Will he be angry because I was late to the theater?' The crisis marked the time both of us really felt, 'No matter what happens, we're in this together.'"[1]

The turning point of a marriage is in a moment of crisis when there is nothing to sustain the two of you but your promise to remain married for a lifetime. It's the point at which a marriage no longer rides on the promise "I do" but "I will."

The payoffs from deciding to stick with it begin almost immediately and are valuable beyond description. Dormen says, "As your commitment matures, intimacy grows steadily, then levels off. You begin to be less focused on your mate, more involved in creating something bigger than the two of you—a family, a home, a business, a spiritual life."[2]

But you'll never discover the "something bigger than the two of you" if you give up. The man or woman who cheats on a spouse has given up. The man or woman who files for divorce to advance a career has given up. The couple who quits forgiving one another has given up. Far too many couples give up far too soon and as a result miss the beauty and meaning their marriage could have.

CHOOSE TO LET YOUR MARRIAGE LIVE

It's like the despondent teenager who contemplates suicide because he has been rejected by the college he wants to attend. A loving and mature adult would put his arm around such a hurting person and say, "Don't do it. There's still so much life ahead. You can't even begin to imagine all the wonderful experiences awaiting you in your twenties and thirties and beyond. As bad as this is, don't take away the possibility of experiencing marriage, parenthood, and a career. I know your heart has been broken, but it will heal. There are other schools and other careers that are worthwhile. Life is still ahead of you."

Yet, when marriages are still in their adolescence, and major disappointments enter the picture, couples assume the only solution is to turn out the lights on the relationship. My advice is, "Don't do it. I know the pain and disappointment are bad right now, but don't kill this relationship. That's not the answer. Your life together is still ahead of you."

Like the teenager who chooses to live, couples need to make a similar commitment to let their marriage live. And the place to begin is by making a mutual commitment to keep your vows, even if you don't feel like doing so at the moment.

This advice doesn't apply just to couples on the verge of splitting up, but also to couples with relatively stable marriages who feel their relationship has grown stale. I issue the same challenge. Go back to your vows. Consider again exactly what you promised each other. Then take the difficult but monumental step of saying, "I'm going to keep my word. I'm going to keep the promises I made on my wedding day. I'm not going to quit."

REFRESHING YOUR MEMORY

Let's assume you accept the idea "if you keep your vows, they will keep you." Let's also assume that in the wedding ceremony you went beyond pledging to share your Visa card and recited more traditional vows. What did you agree to?

"Will you take this person to be your wedded spouse, to live with according to God's law in the holy state of matrimony? Will you love, comfort, honor and keep (him/her), in sickness and in health? And, forsaking all others, will you keep yourself only unto (him/her), so long as you both shall live?"

If we can get past the Elizabethan English, what we discover is that the two of you agreed to something rather remarkable. In fact, it's one of the most profound, incredible, and wondrous contracts two people ever enter into in this life (even beyond Apple and IBM sharing computer information). To what have you signed on in this binding contract?

I Chose of My Own Free Will to Marry This Person

You were asked by the minister if you wanted "to take this person to be your wedded spouse." All you had to say was "No thanks," and the whole thing would have ended right then. But you said, "I do."

It's a sign of both maturity and character to live up to the choices we make. Watch little children at an ice cream counter trying to choose from the thirty-one flavors. They pace the floor, their little noses pressed against the glass to get a closer look, the "I need to make this count" expression on their face. After much agonizing, the choice is finally made. But the real fun starts when the clerk hands them the cones. Inevitably, one of the children will say, "Oh no. I wish I had gotten what you got." The child sits down, face downcast, and reluctantly eats his ice cream cone, consumed with remorse that he didn't order blue moon instead of peanut butter crunch.

Married couples often do the same thing. They make a free and uncoerced choice to marry one person and then spend the rest of their lives lamenting the fact they didn't marry someone else. They miss the one opportunity given to them for happiness because they won't accept the responsibility of their own choice.

You and I promised our mates that we were making this choice of our own free will. We said we were doing it in all sincerity and truth. We need to reaffirm that choice. We need to quit window-shopping, looking in the rearview mirror, or staring in envy at someone else's husband or wife, and accept the gift we have been given.

Suzanne, who came from a troubled home, had serious trouble making commitments. She would swing back and forth from wanting to work out her problems with her husband to deciding to remove all her things from the house at night. I tried to help her see it was her choice to marry Philip and that for her own personal stability and character she needed to stay with that choice. She said she would. Then she changed her mind. Then she changed it back. Ultimately she divorced her husband and, soon after the decree was granted, married another man.

You chose your mate of your own free will. The secret of contentment is to celebrate that choice, to treat it with honor, and to put out of your mind forever the idea you'd be happier with someone else. Why? Because you promised you would. And, if you continue to second-guess yourself, you will blow the only real chance you have to find joy and satisfaction in your marriage.

I Choose to Live according to God's Law of Love

We promised "to live with (our spouse) according to God's law in the holy state of matrimony." My belief about the number one problem in most troubled marriages might surprise you. It isn't sex. It isn't money. It isn't the in-laws. It's that couples have left God out of their relationship.

Alexander Solzhenitsyn, the famous Russian author and historian, was forced from his native land in the 1970s and immigrated to the United States. His address in 1978 to the graduating class of Harvard is regarded by many as one of the most significant addresses of the twentieth century. He told the graduates that day that the entire history of this century, with all its wars and famines and revolutions, could be summarized in one simple statement: "Men have forgotten God." The press ridiculed him, and the intellectual community at Harvard scoffed at his remarks, but he was absolutely right.

Marriage is simply a microcosm of human relationships. Just as nations suffer pain and upheaval when they forget God, so do men and women who try to live together without God.

Jesus said, "Haven't you read…that at the beginning the Creator 'made them male and female,' and said, 'For this reason a man will leave his father and mother and be united to his wife, and the two will become one flesh? So they are no longer two, but one. Therefore what God has joined together, let man not separate.'"[3] Did you notice that last point? What God has "joined together."

Although I have officiated at numerous weddings, I've never married anyone. God does that; I simply act as his representative. I have no power to take two separate humans and, by reciting a ritual, turn them into "one flesh." Only God has that power.

That precise point was driven home to a couple I know when they learned after the honeymoon that their wedding license was invalid. The minister who had performed the ceremony had flown in from out of state and had failed to register with the county. So the couple had to go through a second ceremony in order to have the license granted. The entire time they were on their honeymoon they weren't legally married.

Were they living in sin during that time? No. Although there was a glitch in the legal system, in the eyes of the Almighty they were husband and wife. God is the one who joined them together the day they exchanged vows.

If it is God who joins people together, if he is the Creator who designed a couple's sexuality and attraction to each other, if he is the Master Architect of human relationships, how can a marriage possibly work that ignores his existence? Yet many troubled marriages assume their relationship is comprised of just themselves. "Just you and me, baby...," the love song goes. That's where trouble so often begins. Couples choose every other basis imaginable for their marriage except the one valid foundation—a spiritual one.

I read with interest the story of a woman who wrote to *Good Housekeeping*, saying, "I still love my ex-husband." The couple had opened a kitchen supply store after they were married, and they had spent so much time on their business that the relationship deteriorated. One day the husband announced he had found someone else and was leaving. But the business demanded that the couple continue to work together throughout the divorce proceedings and even after he remarried.[4]

Their story is a tragedy. They built their marriage around a business, not God. Even though the husband divorced his wife, married another, and was soon to be a father, the first wife still loved him. She did so because God had joined them together, and they were one flesh. You can't tear apart one flesh without wounds. Even then, the longing is to be whole again. This woman wasn't neurotic or unbalanced because she still loved her husband. What she was feeling was the natural result of marriage.

When we lived in the Southwest, we met a couple who had purchased a home in a new subdivision out in the desert. It had everything they had ever wanted: spacious rooms, stylish exterior, lovely landscaping.

They woke up one day to find their pictures hanging at an angle. Soon they noticed the windows wouldn't shut tight. Finally cracks began snaking up the living room walls. They called the contractor in a tizzy. Their dream home was falling apart by the hour.

It turned out that their house had been built on a "wash," a dry riverbed that floods only during the rainy season, but the ground can be unstable. Every home in that subdivision experienced the same problems. The contractor eventually filed bankruptcy, and dozens of families were forced to abandon their homes because the foundations were inadequate to support the weight of the structures.

Couples who forget their pledge to "live according to God's law in the holy state of matrimony" are building their homes in a wash. Does that mean they'll divorce? Not necessarily. Does it mean they'll never be happy? No, they may work out a good relationship. But they will never know the full meaning and beauty of marriage unless they base it on having God as Lord and Master of their relationship.

What is God's law for marriage? Jesus defined it in surprisingly simply terms: "'Love the Lord your God with all your heart and with all your soul and with all your mind.' This is the first and greatest commandment. And the second is like it: 'Love your neighbor as yourself.'"[5]

God's law for marriage is to love him first and foremost and then to love each other as much as we love ourselves. What is love? "Love is patient, love is kind. It does not envy, it does not boast, it is not proud. It is not rude, it is not self-seeking, it is not easily angered, it keeps no record of wrongs. Love does not delight in evil but rejoices with the truth. It always protects, always trusts, always hopes, always perseveres."[6]

Whenever I look at this list, I think, "Whoa. I'm supposed to do all that? I wake up so grouchy when I don't get seven full hours of sleep that I need to be put into a containment tank till 9:00 a.m. Yet I'm supposed to be patient, kind, and nonenvious every day of my life? Not!"

That's precisely the point. We can't love another individual in the truest sense of the word unless we are in a relationship with God. He gives me the ability to override my selfish, cranky, and stubborn personality when I allow his love to flow through my life.

I've seen that type of love lived out in marriages. Steven and Sara have been married for nearly forty years. For most of her adult life, Sara has lived with chronic rheumatoid arthritis. She has had virtually every socket and joint in her body replaced with aluminum or plastic to ease her pain. She has not had an hour free of pain in the last two decades.

Her husband has stayed with her through all these years. He literally has to lift her up from her chair and help her sit down. She can go nowhere without him. For years he's had to do all the cooking, cleaning, and grocery shopping. He's logged more hours in waiting rooms while surgeons have worked on her frail body than he can remember. But I've never heard him complain. Come to think of it, I've never heard her complain either.

What's kept them together all these years? The love described by the apostle Paul. Early in their lives they dedicated their marriage to the Creator, and they have remained loving and faithful to one another because of the love and faithfulness of God's character.

Wedding vows that fail to include promises to live according to God's design for marriage aren't complete. They may be good intentions, but chances are they won't be adequate to face problems such as Steven and Sara have.

I Choose to Treat My Spouse as a Person of Value

"Will you love (him/her), comfort (him/her), honor and keep (him/her), in sickness and in health?" That question cuts to the core issue of how we will view the person we're committing to spend the rest of our life with.

A clever burglar once entered a department store after hours. His goal was not to steal the merchandise but to create chaos by switching the price tags on scores of items. Fine French perfume was now marked $1.95, while men's socks sold for $435.00. Leather shoes were a bargain at $.59 while umbrellas would set you back $265.00 plus tax. It was days before the store could reopen, because every item had to be checked to make sure it was marked with its proper value.

One way to disrupt or even destroy a marriage is to fail to treat our mates according to their true value. When we belittle, criticize, ignore, neglect, or demean our husband or wife, we take fine French perfume and sell it for the price of a pair of men's socks. When respect goes, love soon exits as well.

I'm surprised how many couples can't understand why they are so unhappy. They spend hours pointing out the faults of their mates, dwelling on their imperfections, and acting as if they are the biggest nuisance of their life, and then they can't understand why the feelings of love just aren't there anymore.

It's because they no longer value the person they are living with. Our minds and hearts listen to what we say and the way we treat our mates, and they respond accordingly. If we love, comfort, and honor another person in our everyday actions, our emotions are going to keep pace.

I'd like to challenge every husband and wife who think they have lost their feelings of love to try the following experiment. For three days treat your mates as if they are of enormous value to you. Go out of your way to show true respect, to listen with real intensity and without interrupting, and to compliment sincerely their strong traits. Keep your critical thoughts to yourself, and, instead, showcase their strengths to your friends and family. Anticipate their needs and put them first. Show affection even when it isn't for the purpose of making love. And give your mates time to relax and find solitude.

I will wager that after three days of acting this way your feelings will undergo a transformation. It's called cognitive dissonance. Our mind won't allow our feelings to exist contrary to our behavior. If we treat someone with love, honor, and respect, we are going to begin feeling it.

I once spent a month with an Irish minister and his wife who were in their late sixties. While he was the guest speaker at our church for four weeks, I was to chauffeur him and his wife around the city. Those four weeks transformed my understanding of marriage.

The love affair that these two had sustained was extraordinary. Wherever they went, he treated her with dignity and respect. While chauffeuring them, I would listen to them talk to one another. Every two or three miles he would ask, "How are you, darling?" "Just fine," she would reply. He was just checking.

I contrast that to a scene my sister witnessed in a department store where she worked. The manager's wife came in and showed her husband a new blouse she wanted to buy. "Why would you buy that?" he said so loud others could hear. "You know you're built like a man." Not surprisingly, they later divorced.

At no time is that attitude of value and respect more difficult to maintain than when a person's health fails. A mate's needs can become overwhelming, and the daily demands a burden. When the couple is no longer able to function in a typical marital relationship, the commitment to value each other is put to the supreme test.

I know two families who were hit hard by Alzheimer's disease. In the first case the wife was afflicted with the disease and eventually had to be institutionalized. When the medical costs began mounting, the husband filed for divorce to protect his assets. He was then relieved of his burden to pay for her costs, and the state was forced to pick up the tab. Whatever his motives were, his wife died a divorced woman. It may have made sense economically, but I wonder how he rationalized away his promise to "love, comfort, honor, and keep her in sickness and in health."

I believe the vow to value our spouses until the day they die is worth sacrificing everything we have, even if it costs us every penny. Marriage is much more than protecting a pension or guarding our IRAs; it's valuing a human being above every other thing on earth. And as the scripture says, where your treasure is, your heart is also.

The second couple responded quite differently. When it

became apparent he was suffering from the disease, his wife said, "We have had a wonderful marriage for all these years. I could not have asked for a better husband. It is now my privilege to care for him. I know if the roles were reversed, he would do the same for me."

What's the difference between the two marriages? One sees their vows as situational pledges, the other as inviolable promises. When you marry, no one can promise that you'll retire rich, healthy, or whole. Your marriage may involve sacrifices that are unimaginable. But the pledge to value the other person, come what may, is what gives a couple the security and confidence to face the future.

I Agree to Be a Faithful Partner until the Day I Die

"And, forsaking all others, will you keep yourself only unto (him/her), so long as you both shall live?" Do you remember saying that?

A radio and television talk show host once asked his audience, "If I were to give you a million dollars, would you agree to let me spend one night with your wife?" Callers were urged to dial a 900 number to register their vote. People who were interviewed on the street gave mixed reactions. It was clear that for a price a surprising number of people would willingly compromise the sexual integrity of their marriage.

But as the talk show host later said, "The right answer is no. Regardless of how you rationalize it, entering into an agreement like that would forever change your marriage. It could never be the same."

He's right. Maintaining integrity and purity in marriage gives it strength and meaning. There is one part of our life together that absolutely no one else on earth has the right to share. It is ours, and ours alone.

Frank Pittman, the author of *Private Lies: Infidelity and the Betrayal of Intimacy*, lists several popular fallacies about adultery that appear in advice columns, supermarket magazines, and even some books on marriage therapy:

Fallacy #1: Most people have affairs. As Pittman points out, surveys indicate that about 50 percent of married men and 20 to 35 percent of married women are unfaithful. That means the majority of married people stay true to their spouses. An article in October, 1993, in the *Chicago Sun Times* suggested the rate of infidelity between couples may be as low as 15 percent.

Fallacy #2: An affair can be good for a marriage and can even revive a dull one. "Wrong," says Pittman. "The truth is most affairs do great damage. Overall, 53 of the 100 adulterous marriages I surveyed ended in divorce. This, in spite of the couples' decision to seek counseling and my own best efforts to help them. By contrast, it is unusual in my practice for nonadulterous marriages to dissolve."

Fallacy #3: The lover is sexier than the spouse. "In my experience, lovers are not necessarily younger or more attractive than the spouse; nor is the affair necessarily about sex. Thirty of the people I surveyed—half men and half women—acknowledged that their sex lives at home were perfectly adequate. It was not sex but a lack of intimacy that compelled them to have an affair."[7]

The author summarizes his research by saying, "If there is one conclusion I can draw, it's that monogamy works. It isn't rare—it's practiced by most people most of the time, and always has been. It isn't difficult—anyone can do it, and only the smallest sacrifices are involved. Monogamy isn't even dull—living without lies and secrets opens you up to being known and understood, and that isn't dull."[8]

The pledge to remain sexually faithful to another person is in your own best interest. It is the only possible arrangement that can offer a lifelong, fulfilling sexual relationship. Everything else has been tried, and it doesn't work.

Whoever owns the copyright to the initial version of the wedding vows had deep insight into human nature. "So long as you both shall live" is the only promise that makes marriage truly marriage. It's the only pledge that guarantees that both of you are truly serious about this union. Anything less than the promise of lifelong commitment is more like going steady.

A sign outside of a Catholic monastery captured this truth: "You only get one chance at life, but if done right, once is enough." You don't need a variety of partners, lovers, or spouses to experience the best life has to offer. It can be done with just one person. In fact, to truly experience life's best, it needs to be with just one person, for keeps.

That permanence gives our children security. It allows us to plan for our future once the children grow up and leave. It offers economic stability to our lives. It gives us the chance to form lasting friendships with others. It allows us to develop family traditions and create memories. The assurance that we will be together for as long as we live allows us to receive all the best things from life.

The wisest king ever to rule also acted perhaps the most foolishly. Solomon of ancient Israel took for himself over a thousand wives, believing that such vast numbers of lovers would offer him the ultimate satisfaction. Listen to his sad conclusion, "I denied myself nothing my eyes desired; I refused my heart no pleasure.…Yet…everything was meaningless, a chasing after the wind; nothing was gained under the sun."[9]

Conclusion

Why should we keep our vows? Because they will keep us from wasting our lives, from squandering the sweetest gifts life can offer, and from coming down to our final days and saying, "It was all so meaningless." God has a better plan for you and me than that sad ending. But we can only discover it if we're willing to keep our promises.

When my father returned home from World War II as a decorated air force pilot, his first words to my mother were "I promised you I'd come home." If you've been struggling with your marriage, let me offer you some good news. Your promises, if kept faithfully, will bring you home, too.

Chapter Five

INVESTING IN THE BONDING MARKET:

How to Re-Pair a Marriage

W hen Adam and Denise separated after five years of marriage, Adam was devastated. He wanted to win Denise back, but he had no idea where to begin. Then an idea hit him. What if they started over by dating again?

Because the tension between them was still high, he began by just calling her. At first she was guarded and defensive, but gradually their conversations lasted longer and longer. Slowly, after dozens of hours on the phone, the tension between them dissipated until Denise admitted one night she actually looked forward to his calls.

After several weeks of cordial conversations, Adam decided it was time to take the next step—to ask her out. It seemed crazy, but he was as nervous dialing her number that day as he had been the first time he called her for a date. The phone rang once, twice, and then Denise was on the line. After stumbling through some introductory niceties, Adam got to the point.

"Denise, I...I was wondering. If you aren't busy Friday night, could I take you out for dinner?"

There was a long pause on the other end. "Adam, I don't know…"

"Denise, look, I'm not going to try anything with you. I promise. All I want to do is take you to a nice restaurant where we could sit and talk face to face, instead of over the phone."

"Are you sure that's all?"

"I promise, that's all."

"Well," she hesitated, "okay. I guess I'll give it a chance this one time."

Adam stayed true to his word and was a perfect gentleman, and they had a wonderful dinner together. Toward the end of the evening Adam reached for her hand as they walked out the door. She didn't try to let go. The exhilaration he had experienced years earlier when he began dating Denise suddenly was back.

That evening was the beginning of a long and slow process of rebuilding their relationship. As trust began to grow between them, they walked arm in arm and sat close to each other at the movies. Over the next several weeks, signs of deeper bonding occurred naturally. When they finally kissed, it was clear their relationship was healing.

Months later Adam and Denise moved back in together and resumed their sexual relationship. Denise now freely admits that if he had pushed for sexual intimacy on that first date, or soon afterwards, it probably would have destroyed their chances of reconciling. But because they took the time and patience to retrace their steps, their marriage was eventually repaired.

THE IMPORTANCE OF BONDING

People who find themselves in a troubled marriage often jump to the faulty conclusion that they married the wrong person. What may, in fact, have happened is that they followed the wrong path toward bonding and ended up with an imperfect pair-bond—an unfortunate mistake, but by no means a fatal one.

The answer is not to trash the marriage but to go back and begin the bonding process again. Dr. Donald Joy, a well-known author and expert on human sexuality and relationships, has written two insightful and fascinating books entitled *Bonding: Relationships in the Image of God* and *Re-bonding: Preventing and Restoring Damaged Relationships.* His research led him to conclude that the bonding process between a husband and wife follows a long, deliberate, and clearly delineated progression. To short-circuit the process can leave a couple feeling little or no attachment to each other.

Joy defines "pair-bonding" in these terms: "By pair-bonding I wish to refer to that exclusive, lifelong, mutually attaching relationship in which a woman and a man form one new entity, a sort of composite, corporate identity and personality. "[1]

THE TWELVE STEPS TO A BONDED MARRIAGE

Joy drew upon the observations of Desmond Morris, a noted researcher who studied both animal and human behavior. Morris concluded that there are twelve sequential steps to the bonding process, each of which carries both physical and emotional implications. Joy offers a description of each stage and what messages might be attached to it:

1. Eye to body. Amazing! Where have you been all my life?...
2. Eye to eye. Involuntarily, I cannot keep my eyes off you, and I do not even know your name.
3. Voice to voice. What was that again? I missed your name....Would I tease you?

4. Hand to hand. Hang on! We're packing through this crowd as one. It's important that we stick together.

5. Arm to shoulder. It's us against the world....

6. Arm to waist. Move closer. We've got a lot to talk about....Tell me we are together in your longest dream.

7. Face to face. "Drink to me only with thine eyes." Don't say anything; I can read everything and you know what I'm thinking too.

8. Hand to head. I've never felt so safe....I'm comfortable with you.

9. Hand to body. I will take care of you, and I accept you with the peculiar shape of your whole body....

10. Mouth to breast. I salute you. You who will be the mother of our children. I myself draw my strength from you; you have formed my sense of identity....

11. Hand to genital. Everything is yours. I've known all along that we were made for each other.

12. Genital to genital. How could I have known that I was created for this moment and for all the moments it guarantees us?[2]

It should be noted that steps ten through twelve, in which sexual contact occurs, should be saved for the sanctity and commitment of marriage. They are appropriate to a honeymoon, not the second date. For a couple to move from step two or three to step eleven or twelve before marriage risks creating an imperfect pair-bond.

WHAT IF WE DIDN'T GET IT RIGHT THE FIRST TIME?

If you think back over your own courtship, your relationship probably followed the order Joy suggests. However, you may have been influenced by the culture into believing that sexual intimacy is important in getting to know another person. But experience shows that pushing the stages too fast is liable to result in an imperfect pair-bond, and with that come problems later in the marriage.

Although for different reasons, the process of bonding was certainly short-circuited in the marriage of Jacob and Leah. Their relationship really began the night they were married, with full sexual intercourse. It's little wonder that Jacob felt little or no love for his wife. Laban's schemes had effectively circumvented the process of bonding. Yet when Jacob later married Rachel as well, the seven years he had invested in their bonding relationship resulted in a strong marriage.

But even strangers, such as Jacob and Leah, have the potential to love each other. Joy offers this encouragement: "I think Tevye was right in *Fiddler on the Roof:* 'My father and my mother said we'd learn to love each other.'"[3] What Joy is saying is that virtually any two people, if both are willing, can learn to love each other by going through the steps of bonding.

The good news for spouses is that you can re-cover any ground you missed when you were dating or engaged, because bonding is not a one-time opportunity; it is a continual process.

After identifying which steps were missed, Joy suggests: "Begin to reinforce and strengthen the bond by going back to the weak point in the development and putting your intimate investment to work on the missed or weak points.

"Remember, finally, that a healthy pair-bond will be one in which all steps are continuously re-played, with a mild excitement which connects the present to your entire intimate history together."[4]

Even couples who have been married for ten, twenty, thirty,

or more years can go back and repeat the process of pair-bonding when their marriage hits a difficult period. They can repeat the most basic and essential steps in building a love relationship— talking, holding hands, walking arm in arm—and finally progress to the sexual act itself. Each physical step represents a new level of intimacy and attachment to each other. Like getting back to the highway exit where they turned off and got lost, couples need to go back to where they went wrong and start over. For those willing to make the effort, the rewards can be enormous. A repaired bond can set the stage for a lifetime of true intimacy and fulfillment in marriage, unlocking its deepest mysteries and gifts.

The noted family psychologist Dr. James Dobson, in a radio interview with Dr. Joy, recounted the day of his father's death when he discovered just how deep the bond between his father and mother had been: "When the emergency room physician came to notify [my] mother that her husband was gone, she asked, 'May I spend some time with my husband?' The physician agreed to prepare the emergency room for her. My mother spent forty-five minutes with my father's body. She stroked his hands, traced the outline of his feet, his face, and kissed him. She was saying good-bye to the body she had known. It was not primarily sexual; it was total knowledge that had sealed their marriage across the years."[5]

DEVELOPING THE RIGHT ATTITUDES

Besides going through the right steps of re-bonding, it's also important that a couple develop the right attitudes toward each other. That calls for disposing of unproductive ideas and focusing on the positive convictions that make bonding possible.

Perhaps the most useless and counterproductive attitude for

a spouse is, "I married the wrong person." As long as we think that, our marriage is going nowhere. As long as we believe we missed Mr. Perfect or Miss Ideal and married Mr. or Miss Second Best instead, we will feel miserable, angry, and trapped.

I can imagine someone saying, "But, Bob, I did marry the wrong person. My mate is lazy, selfish, inconsiderate, dull, unattractive, hot-tempered, and eats too much!" Your description of your partner's character flaws and appearance may be absolutely right on all counts. But you still have to give up the idea that you married the wrong person, because as long as you insist your mate isn't right for you, he or she never will be.

The Power of a Changed Perspective

Think about it. What good does it do to label your spouse as "the wrong person"? Will it change him or her? Will it give either of you the desire and energy to work on your marriage? Will it bring out the best in your mate?

Dwelling on the belief you married the wrong person sets up a hopeless situation. If your mate is wrong for you, then it's a mistake to stay together. That opens the door to divorce and infidelity.

Instead, do something radical. Today, this very hour, give up once and for all the idea you married the wrong person. Period. Permanently delete that data from your emotional computer, because it's the only way you can get back on track as a couple.

The power of a changed perspective can hardly be overstated. Bob Wieland is a Vietnam war veteran who lost both legs in a land mine explosion. As Bob charged across an open field to pick up a wounded comrade, he stepped on a land mine designed to disable a multiton armored tank.

Bob had ample reason to feel sorry for himself. Prior to being drafted, he was an all-star college baseball player destined for the major leagues. The moment he stepped on the land mine he went from being over six feet tall to thirty-six inches tall. His career in baseball was finished—forever.

But Bob had one thing going in his favor. He refused to give in to despair. He refused to believe his dream of being a professional athlete was over. And five years after his wounds in Vietnam, he won the world weightlifting title in the bench press. With only half a body, he lifted over three hundred pounds.

However, more setbacks were ahead. In an incredible decision, the judges later stripped him of the title because of a technicality. What had he done wrong? He wasn't wearing shoes the day he won the world title.

But Bob is a man who refuses to give up. Instead of giving in to self-pity, he set out on a remarkable venture. He decided he would become the first man to crawl on his hands across the United States. It took him three years and eight months, but Bob Wieland pulled himself from the Pacific Ocean to the Atlantic, one hand at a time.

I share Bob's story because people caught up in the idea that they've married the wrong person can so easily lose perspective. Their anger, self-pity, and bitterness can blind them to the possibilities that still exist in their marriage.

Describe Your Spouse As His or Her Best Friend Would

Often our handicap is our negative attitudes. I challenge you to momentarily stop the tape inside your head that constantly repeats, "I married the wrong person," and, instead, write down all the positive things your spouse's best friend would say about him or her. What different spin would the friend put on the traits that so irritate you? What you describe as boring, the friend might call stable. What you say is stinginess, another might compliment as frugality. What you label as obnoxious, someone else might call being the life of the party.

The truth is, in the beginning you probably were your spouse's best friend and saw his or her personality in the same positive light. It's time to go back and look at your spouse with fresh eyes. When you look again at your husband or wife with respect and esteem, the positive characteristics will again emerge.

Drop the Excuses

Many people actually find their identity in suffering. They have grown so accustomed to feeling sorry for themselves and using excuses for not investing in their marriage that the idea of giving up those excuses is absolutely terrifying. Strange as it sounds, people may actually find comfort in the idea they have a horrible spouse. It gives them someone to criticize and keeps the attention deflected from their own shortcomings. It conveniently excuses their own lack of love and unselfishness and offers an escape route from the hard work of building a marriage.

Jana went through life telling her friends, "You know, people warned me that I should never marry Samuel. I wish I had listened to them." Apparently it never dawned on Jana that she was no real treat to live with either. In fact, of the two, Samuel was far more psychologically and emotionally healthy. But Jana's beliefs kept her from having to face the truth that she was deeply scarred, emotionally immature, and selfish.

Dropping our excuses can be frightening. What will I find if I face reality? What if I'm the failure? What if no one truly does love me? Those are legitimate fears. But again the reality is, there is no love without risk. If you are going to experience true love and intimacy in marriage, you're going to have to risk being vulnerable.

Many inmates fear parole more than prison. They know what it's like to live in a confined cell, to follow a prescribed regimen, and to have someone else order their lives for them day after day. But the idea of hitting the streets, finding a job, and adjusting to society can be terrifying. That is partially why so many convicts return to the penitentiary just a few years after their release.

We also can be so scared of true intimacy and bonding that we won't give up the idea we married the wrong person. But that's where faith and risk taking make the difference between existing and living, cohabiting and becoming one flesh.

The Courage to Back over the Cliff

I remember a time I was forced to face a persistent fear. I was working on staff at the church I grew up in, an inner city church that runs an aggressive summer program for kids. That summer we decided to go mountain climbing.

I have no idea why I agreed to go on this apparently suicidal venture to the Rocky Mountains. When we reached the remote base camp high in the mountains, I looked up at the gray, jutting peaks of the Sangre de Cristo mountains—and gulped.

We spent the first day in camp acclimating to the high altitude air. No problem. The second day we spent playing search and rescue. Great fun. The third day we put on belts and helmets and climbed trees. A bit scary, but manageable. The fourth day they informed us we were going to rappel from a 160-foot cliff—backwards. Wait a minute.

The morning of the "big climb" we had to drag several of the kids—members of the high school basketball team—from their tents. A good friend of mine, who shares my fear of heights, sat dejectedly outside his tent muttering, "I'm going to die today. This is my last day on earth and no one cares." He was serious.

We trudged up the backside of the cliff like condemned men

on our way to execution. No one said a word. Occasionally you would see tears, from both men and women, but the long death march continued.

When we reached the top of the cliff, we walked out onto a narrow ledge and were told to sit down. From here we would literally jump off the mountain.

"Who would like to be first?" the mountain guide asked with a smile. The group sat silent. He might as well have asked, "Who would like to be the first to plunge to his death in screaming agony?"

I was single at the time and decided that I had lived a good life. I had no regrets that today it was ending. Rather than watching others fall to their deaths and end as a puff of smoke on the canyon floor, I decided to go first. As I stood trembling on the ledge of the mountain that sunny Colorado afternoon while mountain guides hooked me into belts and webbing, I had an occasion to review my life. The nineteen years had been good. My parents, friends, and family would miss me. But there would be life insurance, of course.

I walked toward the edge of the cliff as the guide gave me final instructions. "Face the mountain, lean over backwards, and begin feeding rope out through your right hand."

Lean backwards? What kind of sick mind would invent a sport like this? Inching my way to the edge of the cliff, I looked up at the sky. Ready or not, heaven would be receiving a new occupant in the next minute or two.

I took a deep breath and leaned back. With my legs straight out in front of me at a perpendicular angle, I began lowering myself over a 160-foot sheer cliff.

I was just a few feet down the mountain when the thought suddenly struck me, "I must still be alive. No white lights or long tunnels yet." I let out a little more rope, then a little more, and finally began pushing away from the mountain, dancing and hopping down the side of the cliff. Elation swept through my soul. "I am alive! I'm actually still alive."

By the time my feet touched the bottom of the canyon, I was transformed. Every cell and fiber in my body seemed to shout with exultation. When I unclipped my belts and looked up at what I had just done, I couldn't believe it was me. Bob Moeller—the coward of withering heights—was no longer afraid. In fact, I've gone on to enjoy rappelling on several occasions since then. So complete was my release that I later spent several summers roofing houses with my dad. I would sit on top of three-story homes and whistle as I nailed asphalt shingles to the roof.

What's the point of this story? Letting go of the idea "I married the wrong person" may be every bit as intimidating as walking backwards off a 160-foot cliff. It may mean that we have to face the fear of being intimate with the person we married. We may have to risk revealing who we are to another human being. We may have to be vulnerable to rejection and hurt in order to discover acceptance and love. Once we step over the cliff and discover we're still alive, it will mean changing the way we see ourselves and the person we married. When we face our fears and don't run from them, we do more than exist; we begin to live.

The Will to Become the Right Person

The idea that we married the "wrong" person presupposes that there was a "right" person for us to marry but we didn't happen to guess correctly the first time around. To believe that we can find happiness with only one special person in all the universe seems a little far-fetched to me. Is there only one house in the entire nation you could live in and be happy? Only one type of car that could bring you satisfaction? One career?

I had a friend during college who was a native of India. His dating efforts in the United States proved frustrating and unsuccessful, so he returned to his home, and his relatives arranged for him to meet a lovely young woman. He had three hours to decide if he wanted to marry her. He did marry her and hasn't quit smiling since. Pure luck? I doubt it. He entered the marriage realizing, as Tevye said in *Fiddler on the Roof*, that they would learn to love each other.

In junior high I had a crush on a girl, although I don't suppose she even knew it. I used to imagine what it would be like to walk her home from school, but my horn-rimmed glasses and bookworm image didn't interest her in the least.

I ran into her again almost twenty years later. I was a pastor making hospital calls, and she was a nurse. When I asked about her life, a look of pain crossed her face. She and her former husband had married right out of high school and traveled all over the country. They had two kids together before they divorced. She was now a single parent trying to make ends meet. While she was a pleasant person, we were very different people. In fact, I wondered what I had seen in her in the first place.

When I was a young man, I thought on several occasions I had found the right person. Somehow, they never got the message I was the right person for them. I remember dating one Miss Ideal only to learn she was seen passionately kissing another young man in the middle of campus. So much for that.

As time went on, I began to understand it was not a matter of me meeting the right person; it was me becoming the right person. As I matured in my self-knowledge and my relationship with God, I began to understand more about the type of person I wanted to spend my life with.

My definition of the right person also changed with the passing seasons of my life. Life is like that. Today you may be thinking you made the wrong choice, but let me encourage you, there are other seasons ahead. And if you are open to building a marriage characterized by honesty, forgiveness, and acceptance, you may make a remarkable discovery. The individual you married can become the most precious person to you in all the world.

Conclusion

I strongly believe that God wants us to honor our marriage vows and spend our lifetime with the same mate. God would not ask us to do such a thing if he didn't build into the plan of marriage the ability to learn to love one another. That's why bonding is an important step in rediscovering our love for each other. Whether or not we believe we married "the right person," God can give us the capacity to become the right people for each other.

I once asked my parents how they made it through fifty years of marriage. They smiled and said, "We just decided we would." In the end, that's what marriage comes down to. When we decide we have married the right person, we have.

Chapter Six

CAN WE TALK?

A couple I had never met before just showed up at my office one day. They were talking divorce. "The problem with Andrew is that he won't talk." The anger and bitterness in Michelle's voice were unmistakable. "See for yourself," she taunted me. "Try having a conversation with him and see if you can get him to say more than fifty words."

Michelle was ready to end the marriage. Her husband appeared to be the quiet type but wasn't completely nonverbal.

I called Andrew a few days later and invited him out to lunch. He gladly said yes. On the way to the restaurant, I rehearsed several questions I would ask him to see if I could get a conversation going. I entered the crowded lunchroom with verbal pliers in hand, ready to pull a conversation out of him.

What happened next surprised even me. Once we were seated and had ordered, I asked Andrew a simple question. For the next hour I rarely got a word in edgewise. He told me about his job, the family he grew up in, his college experiences, his car, and his love for Michelle. He desperately wanted to save the marriage but had resigned himself that it was probably over.

On the way back to the office I realized what was going on. It wasn't that Andrew couldn't communicate; he had nearly talked my leg off. It was that Andrew couldn't talk to Michelle. Perhaps after losing one too many verbal firefights with his more articulate wife, Andrew had decided life was safer in the bunker of silence and withdrawal.

WHAT MEN REALLY WANT FROM THEIR WIVES

Marriages can flounder for a number of reasons—money problems, emotional behavior, premarital sexual activity, in-law interference, and a variety of other causes. But they all share this characteristic: The couple can't talk to each other. They can't process their anger, resolve conflicts, or share their inmost feelings in an atmosphere of love, respect, and acceptance. As the pain of living together increases, and their ability to communicate diminishes, the marriage gradually dies.

Dr. Lois Ledierman Davitz, author of *Living in Sync: Men and Women in Love*, conducted a study of four hundred divorced men between the ages of twenty and forty-five, whose marriages had lasted anywhere from three months to twenty years. The study focused on finding the primary reasons men divorce their wives. The results surprised the researchers. It was not problems with money, sex, children, or household duties that the men say broke up their marriages.

"What virtually every man in our study cited as decisive to the failure of the relationship was the lack of companionship," says Davitz. "In fact, the men who were planning to marry someone new invariably described her as 'my best friend.'"[1]

What goes into making a wife feel like a best friend?

"'Communication in friendship' is one of the first things men looked for in a new relationship," say the researchers.[2] The problem is men see communication as a by-product of a shared activity, while women see it as the activity itself.

According to Davitz, and I believe she's right, the way to begin reconstructing communication in marriage is by doing things together. It may not be best to start your road back to reconciliation by scheduling a summit meeting in the living room where you two are going to hash out everything that's bothered you for the last two years or two decades. As professional diplomats can tell you, wars often start after failed summits.

Instead, think back to your courtship days. Weren't many of your best conversations on dates where you did something you both enjoyed? Perhaps it was going to a park or concert, or skiing together. Your conversation grew out of your common activity.

"To be fair," Davitz says, "these [divorced] men probably shared this kind of camaraderie with their wives early in their relationships. Yet somehow, as the stresses of jobs, children and other responsibilities intruded, couples drifted away from this pattern of communication in friendship."[3]

THREE WAYS TO START TALKING AGAIN
So what's the way back? She offers three ideas:

1. Let your communication grow spontaneously out of the things the two of you do together.
2. Go easy on the heart-to-heart talks.
3. Laugh together.[4]

There's an old Southern adage that says, "Dance with who brought you." If it was bowling, listening to good music, or walking by the ocean that first drew you together and gave you an opportunity to share your hearts, then go back and do it again. Or find new activities that allow both of you to feel more at ease together. The time will come when more serious and substantial discussion will be needed, but your level of personal pain and frustration may be so high at the moment that it's simply not possible to make progress that way.

ANIMAL INSTINCTS IN COMMUNICATION

Perhaps the most difficult aspect of communication in marriage is learning to solve conflicts. Although some couples seem to have a natural ability to resolve hard issues, most of us have to work at it. Unless we learn how to manage conflict in our relationship, it ends up managing us.

I'll never forget a scene I witnessed as a young boy in our neighborhood one summer day. I was playing in our front yard when I heard shouting start across the street. The front door to a neighbor's home burst open. A woman marched to her car, jerked open the driver's side door, then stopped to hurl one final epithet at her husband. Satisfied her insult had found its mark, she then got into the car. She cranked the engine, threw it into reverse, and hit the accelerator. The automobile shot backward out the driveway, careened across the street, and ran smack dab into a tree. The woman never got out of the car to inspect the damage but instead jammed the car into drive and screeched away down the street.

Obviously this couple was having problems communicating. A dented bumper and a gash in the trunk of a tree were witnesses to that truth. But it was more than a reckless argument; it was an example of what conflict management experts call avoidance. While she obviously didn't avoid the tree, she did avoid staying at home to resolve the conflict. It was easier to flee than fight.

Avoidance is just one of five different methods of communication that couples use when they're trying to resolve conflict.

The other methods are competition, accommodation, negotiation, and collaboration.

Norman Shawchuck is a conflict management consultant
who has written extensively on the ways human beings attempt
to resolve problems when they "confligere (the Latin word for
conflict, which literally means 'to strike together')."[5]

As a helpful way of organizing these ideas, he's given animal
names to each of these communication styles—the Shark, the
Teddy Bear, the Turtle, the Fox, and the Owl. They describe the
predictable behavior of humans when faced with a conflict, and
they may give you insight into yourself and your mate.

Meet Jaws in Person

1. The Shark (The Competitor). Sharks are competitors
who see each marital argument, whether it's over the checkbook
or the electric bill, as a win or lose situation. And they intend to
win. Sharks tend to be domineering, aggressive, and agreeable to
any solution—as long as it's the one they want.

Sharks tend to get what they want one way or another.
They're willing to use persuasion, power plays, or coercion to
reach their goals. They will shout louder, sulk longer, or withhold sex. All is fair in love and war to a Shark. Watching a Shark
in action isn't pretty, but being on the wrong end of their pearly
white teeth is even worse, as any surfer will tell you.

Margaret was a Shark. She controlled her husband and
everyone else in her world with her temper. To keep the peace,
and to save himself from the wrath of Mrs. Jaws, her husband
would just give in whenever her gray fin started circling in the
water.

There's a problem with a win/lose approach to communication. Even if you win, someone else loses. In marriage, that
someone else happens to be the person who should be the most

important, cherished person in your life. When a Shark is allowed to rule a marriage, subsurface anger builds, decisions are not enthusiastically carried out, and a dangerous dependency builds around the strong-willed individual, according to Shawchuck.

The subsurface anger is the part that worries me most. My first year out of seminary I pastored a Midwestern church that had a considerable number of senior citizens, including Walter. Walter was known throughout the church as Mr. Milquetoast. He barely spoke above a whisper. He gave generously to offerings. He attended a Bible study on Thursday mornings at the church.

His first wife died, and in his eighties he remarried a lady who had a much stronger personality than he. I was shocked and horrified one night to learn on the evening news that his second wife had been brutally murdered with a crowbar. The hunt was on for the perpetrator of this terrible crime.

About a week later, just before turning in for the night, I again switched on the ten o'clock news. The lead story immediately caught my attention: "Tonight the police arrested a suspect in the murder of an elderly woman."

I expected to see a tough young guy with a four-day beard and a leather jacket, perhaps flashing a gang signal, being led out of a squad car. Instead, the camera showed a hunched-over, eighty-eight-year-old man in bifocals and slippers, shuffling into police headquarters. It was Walter!

Walter was convicted of first-degree murder and sentenced to, yes, life in prison. The police believed the motive behind the killing was his simmering anger at his second wife for allegedly distributing some of his savings to her children.

Although few couples resort to this extreme method of solving conflict, a win/lose dynamic is destructive to any couple's chances for long-term happiness. The person who loses all the time is eventually going to get sick of it.

Peace at Any Price

2. The Teddy Bear (The Accommodator). These people are easy to like because their life's ambition is to keep peace and make everyone happy. They see the world in terms of lose/win; that is, they are consistently willing to give up their rights to accommodate someone else's desires.

So what's wrong with that? Doesn't that make for an ideal partner? Actually, no. The problem with Teddy Bears is that they never solve problems; they just yield to other people to avoid any further conflict. These people are the "peace at any price" delegation. Just as history has shown that appeasement never leads to lasting peace, constantly surrendering principles and convictions in marriage leads ultimately to unhappiness and a breakdown of intimacy.

Using accommodation to solve conflicts in marriage ultimately gives the victors an unreal sense of their own rightness. And the Teddy Bears end up plagued by feelings of inauthenticity and falsehood for acting so cheerful and easygoing when in fact they are miserable and angry. They grow weary of frantically trying to keep the relationship together, which exacts a high price on their own emotional and spiritual health. The problems they've swept under the carpet for years come back to haunt them. Their self-esteem plummets from constantly accepting the blame for arguments and problems that were not their fault. Eventually, the emotional stuffing starts to fall out of a Teddy Bear.

Sybil was close to a nervous breakdown when we met her several years ago out West. Her husband traveled frequently and expected her to cope with the demands of sick children, running a house, and giving him time off to play with his buddies. If the baby cried during the night, it was just expected that Sybil would be the one to get up. If Sybil's husband wanted to go away for the weekend fishing, it was up to her to pack the suitcase. If she ever objected to his carefree lifestyle, he would shout back, "Don't forget, I'm the one earning the money in this family." Meekly she would back down and work harder.

Sybil is a prime candidate for emotional exhaustion or an affair. Whenever she and her husband argue, he successfully manages to shift the blame for his own eternal adolescence and irresponsible behavior to her. Unfortunately, she accepts it. She honestly believes that's the loving thing to do. But they can't be happily married as long as Sybil continues her codependent behavior and allows him to play emotional tennis, constantly slamming guilt and blame onto her side of the court.

Let's Split the Difference

3. The Fox (The Negotiator). The Fox is a specialist at compromise. In marriage, Foxes are usually able to cut the pie in such a way that it appears the other person got the biggest slice. They view relationships in terms of everyone-wins-a-little/everyone-loses-a-little. They genuinely want to see a compromise reached with their husband or wife, and they'll use a little gentle persuasion or manipulation to get the other person to sign on. Their bargaining skills are used to defuse potentially explosive situations in marriage, and for the most part they can do it with a smile. The problem with this particular style of communication and conflict resolution is that everyone goes away half-satisfied, the commitment to the solution is only half-hearted, and the same conflict will arise later because it's only half-solved.

Edward's in-laws didn't like him. When he and his wife would visit her parents, they would deliberately ignore him.

They treated him as if he were an intrusion into their family. They refused to acknowledge any of his professional accomplishments. Edward told his wife about his deep hurt and sense of rejection. Instead of dealing with her parents in a direct fashion about their behavior, she suggested that he accompany her only every other time she visited them. That would cut in half the number of painful experiences he had to absorb from them.

That's the problem with negotiation as a primary means of talking a problem out. The solution rarely gets to the root of the problem; it simply makes it easier to live with.

What Problems?

4. The Turtle (The Avoider). These people are by no means an endangered species. They exist in marriages everywhere. When a problem pops up in marriage, their strategy is simply to pretend it doesn't exist. They may refuse to open bills they can't pay, or fail to return calls to angry neighbors. They see the world in terms of a lose/lose situation. They are so fearful of conflict that they become passive and withdrawn.

Turtles are frustrating people to live with. They won't cooperate in defining the problem, or seeking a solution, or implementing an agreement. They have very little emotional investment in the relationship. Their emotional gears are stuck in neutral. When a husband or wife is trying to communicate with a Turtle, the Turtle will remain silent, or say little, or actually get up and leave the premises.

Norman Shawchuck tells the story of a couple he counseled who were having marital problems. The wife insisted on having all the family pets sleep in the same bed with them. There were at least two poodles and a cat on the queen-sized bed at all times. When the husband expressed his discontent, she just disregarded him. It was her method of avoiding intimacy with him. As long as there were representatives of the wild kingdom on their bed, nothing else too wild was going to happen.

Turtles tend to be heavy into denial. They say nothing when their partners make a reckless financial decision or come home boasting about the new woman at the office they took out to lunch. When Turtles find empty whiskey bottles in the garage, they simply throw them away and ask no questions.

Such passivity takes its toll on a marriage. Apathy eventually saps the energy and the excitement from the relationship. The Claus von Bulow trial involved a millionaire husband who purportedly administered an overdose of insulin to his wife to collect her estate and clear the way for marrying a mistress. Testimony at the trial confirmed the fact that von Bulow's wife had told him he could keep a mistress if he wanted to, as long as he was discreet about it. Perhaps the only statement more damaging to a marriage than "I hate you" is "I don't care."

Come, Let Us Reason Together

5. The Owl (The Collaborator). According to folklore, owls are wise creatures. Wise couples will adopt an "owlish" style of co-laboring toward solutions in their marriage. Owls desire a win/win solution to problems and disagreements. That's why they are willing to "co-labor," hence the term "collaboration," until mutually satisfying resolutions are reached to sticky and difficult issues.

The Owl is perhaps just the opposite of a Turtle. Owls are willing to stay up and talk a problem out rather than retreat to the solitude of a bedroom or a night on the couch. They truly have the interests of both people at heart, and they see conflict as an opportunity to strengthen their marriage, not destroy it. When Owls solve problems, they tend to remain solved. They don't keep reappearing under some different guise. When a husband and wife collaborate and are committed to implementing the agreements they reach, they learn to trust each other, and they emerge a more thoroughly committed and satisfied couple.

The question in any marriage is not, "How can we avoid conflicts?" but "How can we learn to resolve them in a way that strengthens our marriage?" The answer to that is collaboration.

How then can a couple regularly apply the principles of collaboration? Shawchuck suggests three important principles.

Get to the Real Issue

Step One: Generate as much useful and valid information as possible.[6]

When a couple approaches a problem in their marriage, they need to see it as an issue to be solved, not a person to be conquered. That requires sharing with each other all the true and relevant information that surrounds the issue. Misconceptions and assumptions have to be filtered out in favor of accurate and reliable facts.

Couples tend to exaggerate in an argument. "You've never remembered a single anniversary since we've been married!" "I always have to be the one to discipline the children." "I can't think of a single nice word you've said to me this week."

An old proverb states, "Never say never and always avoid saying always." It's often difficult in the heat of battle to stop and sift out the wheat from the chaff or distinguish between the marble and the manure, but it's necessary if true conflict resolution is going to take place.

Janis Long Harris, a contributing editor for *Today's Christian Woman*, gives an example of the way exaggeration can quickly get out of hand: "If I'm having a bad day, for example, and Paul comes home from work an hour late, I'm capable of turning what might seem to be a minor offense into a serious character disorder. 'There he goes again,' I might huff to myself. 'I can never count on him to be home on time. He's unreliable. I should have recognized this flaw in his character when he was always late when we were dating. Whatever possessed me to marry this man?'"[7]

Collaboration requires putting those thoughts out of our minds. Such exaggerations aren't true, and they don't do anything to solve the problem. Dismiss them each time they try to grab hold of your thinking process. A Chinese proverb says, "That the birds of worry and care fly about your head, this you cannot change. But that they build nests in your hair, this you can prevent."

What if he was late because he had a flat tire? Or was caught in a traffic jam? Or stopped to buy a rose? Is that a character flaw worthy of jeopardizing the marriage? Exaggerations are by nature silly. When we're tempted to overreact to a problem in our marriage, it's better to step back and laugh at ourselves. We're being ridiculous, and we can't generate valid and useful information when we're being unreasonable.

To gain useful data we need to ask each other questions such as, "What hurt you most about what I did?" "What's your greatest need at this moment?" "What's the issue behind this issue?" Counselors distinguish between the "presentation issue" and the "primary issue." A husband or wife will often bring up a problem that isn't the real issue, just because it's safer to talk about. It's a defense mechanism we use to make sure the other person is really open to our feelings and hurts before we disclose them. Or, we may be just too fearful to bring up the real subject, so we only hint at what we need.

For example, a spouse who is feeling like a failure at work may come home and ask why the house is such mess or why the kids aren't dressed better. The other spouse might respond to the hurt or anger by complaining about the other's relatives. Couples who can't get past the presentation issue to discuss the primary issue will seldom solve their conflicts. To make progress requires patience, sensitivity, and an openness to the truth.

When I was a pastor, I would sometimes take a serious hit over a trivial matter. A person's criticism would sting, and I'd be left wondering, "What did I do to deserve this?" Over the course of several years I learned a basic rule: When the stimulus (my actions) doesn't fit the response (someone's severe criticism), something else is at work. A man who constantly criticized my sermons for months eventually confided to me that his wife had asked for a divorce. All those months he had been trying to get my attention but didn't have the courage to tell me what was really on his heart.

Couples can get angry or upset over a relatively minor problem, but it's not the real problem. Successful communication in marriage requires putting our flamethrowers away and attempting instead to generate valid and useful information.

Give Each Other the Right to Choose

The second step that Shawchuck recommends in developing the skills of a collaborator is to give each person the right to make free and informed choices about the future.[8] People don't enjoy having solutions forced on them. To build lasting harmony in a marriage, each person must be given the authority and freedom to make decisions as to how the problem will be solved.

One way to begin is to break the larger problem down into small pieces, particularly if it's an issue that continually creates conflict between you. Search for the areas you already agree on. Then use those smaller agreements to work toward crafting an overall settlement. Let's say the argument concerns housekeeping chores. It won't solve the issue for one person to announce,

"From now on, you're doing the dishes and shopping for groceries, and I'm paying the bills and doing the yard. And that's final."

The only choice the other person has is to take it or leave it. Not very inviting. Far better to say, "Look, there's more work around here than either of us can handle alone. Let's discuss which chores each of us enjoys doing. Then, we'll work together on dividing up the remainder. What's your first choice of jobs? Then I'll share mine."

How important is it that couples learn to successfully negotiate smaller issues? Researchers at the University of Denver's Center for Marital and Family Studies set up mock living room labs and used sophisticated monitoring devices to study the behavior of couples trying to resolve conflict. The director of the project, Dr. Howard J. Markman, claims that love and attraction don't naturally diminish over time; they are attacked and worn down by negative feelings that grow out of destructive fights.[9]

Dr. Clifford Notarius of Catholic University explains, "It matters less what couples fight about than how they fight about it."[10] I've had couples sit in my office and say, "It's hopeless. He (or she) is never going to change." That type of pessimism almost guarantees no progress.

Let me stress again, problems in marriage are issues to be solved, not people to be conquered. There is almost a sense of exhilaration when a couple can solve a problem together.

Cheryl and I once spent an entire day tackling our garage. It was actually dangerous to open the door. We seriously considered buying a St. Bernard before starting the project so that if we were buried by an avalanche of old tires, baby cribs, and college textbooks, we could be located before nightfall. But when the day was over and the dust finally settled, we stood arm in arm admiring the intimidating task that we had conquered together. It was a General Foods gourmet coffee moment for both of us.

Work Together

The final suggestion Shawchuck makes for developing the skill of collaboration is basically common sense: People support solutions they have helped create.[11] One-sided decisions or executive orders issued from the top don't cut it in a marriage. Both partners need to feel that they are an equal member of the decision-making process and their input matters.

The journal I work for once printed a cartoon of ancient laborers groaning as they pulled a huge block of stone toward a pyramid. Riding atop the massive boulder was the Egyptian taskmaster. Below, the caption read, "Remember fellas, we're all members of the same team."

Problems in a marriage aren't solved when one partner sits on top of the boulder and shouts orders to the other. Partners need to bear together the burden of solving the problem and then implementing the solution.

Keith and Marta were having problems with their phone bill. Each month it exceeded two hundred dollars. After several unproductive arguments over money, budgets, and phone calls, they decided to attack the problem together. Keith agreed to carry change with him wherever he went, instead of charging the calls on his credit card. That brought discipline to the length and frequency of his calls. Marta agreed to write more letters to friends and relatives, instead of picking up the phone to call whenever she missed them. They set a target of a hundred dollars per month for phone service and then checked with each other frequently for support and accountability. Within a month's time the phone bill had been cut in half. Why? Because they had both contributed to the solution, and as a result both were motivated to implement it.

SECRETS OF HAPPY COUPLES

So how can you lower the decibel rating in the argument to discover the areas where you do agree? Scott Winokur in his article "What Happy Couples Do Right" suggests four essential principles of a collaborative approach to conflict resolution.[12] In order to make free and informed choices to resolve problems, couples need to observe the following rules:

1. Don't run from strife. "Even happy couples argue, but they don't shut each other out." They listen closely to each other to make sure they understand what the other person is saying.

2. Give up on the put-downs. "Contempt can kill a marriage. Just a simple look of disdain or condescension can crush the spirit of another person." Such shame-based behavior leaves wounds that can take days, or years, to heal. Even in the throes of a loud argument, respect for each other needs to be maintained.

I've never been amused by the old Jackie Gleason series, "The Honeymooners." The nonstop put-downs, insults, and even veiled threats of violence ("One of these days, Alice, smack, right in the kisser!") are hardly humorous. A couple that savages each other for eighteen hours a day, ridiculing each other's appearance, career, and in-laws, hardly has time at the end of the day to be reconciled and revive intimacy.

Winokur points out, "Thriving couples are polite to each other....Unhappy couples, on the other hand, may employ such nasty tactics as character assassination ('You don't want a better job because you're lazy') and hostile mind reading ('You don't call when you're going to be late because you don't care that I stay awake worrying')."[13]

For a couple to make free and informed choices the atmosphere needs to be cleansed of the toxic pollutants of contempt and ridicule. Respect, grace, and politeness need to be the air that collaborative couples breathe.

3. Don't dwell on downers. Collaborative couples are able to put the brakes on an argument before it careens off the highway and leaves them both seriously injured. Winokur points out, "Clashes for well-matched couples will go on only so long before one partner refocuses the exchange...or calms the other down."

Let's face it. We all know we can either feed a fight or starve it. Proverbs 17:14 offers us this bit of advice for feuding folks, "Starting a quarrel is like breaching a dam; so drop the matter before a dispute breaks out."

Collaboration is a discipline. It requires both mates backing away from the temptation to throw at each other everything they can think of in order to win the fight.

Several years ago a classic work on marriage entitled *The Intimate Enemy* warned that there are some statements we can never take back again. "I never wanted to marry you in the first place!" "I don't care whether you live or die." "I wish I had married a real man so I could experience good sex at least once." Couples should never say such statements as these because the damage may last for a lifetime.

Like a boxing ring with carefully prescribed boundaries and rules, collaborative couples can fight, but they refuse to hit below the belt or throw dirty punches. When the buzzer sounds, they put aside their gloves, shake hands, and leave the arena as friends.

4. Think like a winner. It's important for collaborative couples to believe they are going to succeed in solving the issues in their lives. They need to enter a discussion with the confidence that as a couple they can overcome whatever they are facing.

Researchers have found that unhappy couples enter into arguments expecting to fail. "[When] unhappily married men and women who hadn't seen each other all day were called together to a lab to discuss a problem, they registered dramatic signs of stress—elevated heart rates, more rapid respiration and increased perspiration. Convinced that irresolvable conflict lies ahead, their bodies shift into distress modes in advance...."[14]

NIPPING IT IN THE BUD:
THE FIVE STAGES OF CONFLICT

A surgeon once told me that most of the cancers he deals with are three-fifths of the way toward taking someone's life before they are diagnosed. Unfortunately, the same is often true of marriages. Problems that should have been handled early on are allowed to grow and fester until they threaten the survival of the relationship.

Is there a way to diagnose problems in the early stages and deal with them before they become life-threatening? Again, Shawchuck believes there is. He maintains, "Once begun, conflict follows a five stage progression. The length of time for any stage may be very short (a few minutes) to very long (several months), but no stage is missed."[15]

If couples are to handle conflict before it manhandles them, they need to recognize these five stages and respond appropriately.

Stage One: Tension Development

A neighbor told me how he and his wife once drove to work without saying a word to each other. Just before dropping his wife off, he said, "Well, what is it? What are you angry about?"

His bewildered wife looked back at him and said, "I'm not angry. I thought you were angry." Then they both laughed, kissed each other, and headed off for a day's work.

What they experienced was tension development, the beginning of any conflict. It's a general uneasiness that something has changed or is out of place. Because it is so subtle, we're often embarrassed to say anything about it. After all, what if there is nothing to it? Won't we look silly for saying anything?

Rarely. Most often if you sense tension, it's because there is tension. If it's brought out into the open and discussed candidly, the problem will likely end right there. If not, the tension will continue—and build.

Stage Two: Role Dilemma

The confusion created by the changing tensions of relationships reaches the next level. As Shawchuck points out, confusion enters the scene, and people are left wondering just where they stand. Their roles are now unclear. As the situation grows more threatening, people tend to say less, not more. Communication quickly fades and gives way to irrational assumptions and prejudices.

David Seamands, the noted author and marriage counselor, tells the story of one of the worst nights of his married life. He and his wife had just purchased a dual-control electric blanket. Somehow the controls on the headboard got rearranged, so each was unknowingly controlling the temperature on the opposite side of the blanket. Because he likes it hot, he cranked up the controls several notches. She likes it cooler at night, so she turned her controls way down. Before long, he was approaching hypothermia; she was being broiled alive.

Roles were well out of hand that night. The higher we turn the tensions, the less we achieve of what we really want.

The solution to role dilemma is still relatively painless compared to allowing the problem to grow. It requires facing the problem, discussing it honestly, and laying it to rest. But if the problem is still left unaddressed, the stakes are raised another notch.

Stage Three: Injustice Collecting

This is the first truly dangerous stage of a conflict, according to Shawchuck. Husbands and wives begin storing their grievances against one another the way gophers stick acorns in their pouches to chew later. Couples sense that things are going to get worse before they get better, so they begin preparing themselves for battle.

By this stage so much negative energy has accumulated that it has to be released before any reconciliation can occur. Couples can remain at this stage for days, weeks, and even years while injuries and hurts continue to be collected on both sides, and the cache of available ammunition grows.

The story is told of a church split in which both sides eventually tried to present their case before the State Supreme Court. Each side argued that it was the rightful owner of the building and properties. The court refused to rule in the case and instead sent it back to the denomination to handle under its own jurisdiction. A lengthy investigation followed. What caused this once-prosperous church to become so viciously divided? The investigation traced the roots of the conflict back to a church banquet in which one man was given a larger slice of ham than another.

Couples can allow relatively minor spats to grow into sizable and potentially dangerous arguments if they practice injustice collecting. At this stage, the raw emotions need to be dealt with before the negative energy can be dispelled and the couple can start discussing the problem reasonably.

Stage Four: Confrontation

This is the stage most of us associate with conflict. Here, "contact" occurs, and everything from angry accusations to shoes can start flying. The focus changes from issues to personalities, and things can become particularly nasty. Police officers will readily admit their most dangerous calls are to domestic arguments.

Confrontation, even when it doesn't involve violence, is still a difficult experience for a marriage to absorb. Shawchuck explains, "Persons are now confronted with a set of less-than-desirable alternatives; they can sever the relationship, attempt to return to the way things used to be, or they can negotiate a new set of expectations and commitments. However, such negotiation is always done under pressure because the person feels there is no other viable alternative."[16]

Have you ever wondered why two people who love each other so much can also fight so hard? The two are actually connected. The more intense and encompassing the relationship, the greater the potential for serious confrontation. Which hurts more? An argument between you and a banker over a discrepancy on your monthly statement, or a shouting match between you and your spouse over a bounced check?

The answer is obvious. You have very little invested in your relationship with the bank (perhaps in more ways than one). You can just withdraw your money and go down the street. But you have your entire emotional, physical, and perhaps spiritual self invested in your relationship with your mate. You can't just close your account and leave, not without paying a tremendous price. That's why confrontations in marriage can get so ugly—the two people are highly invested in each other. That's also why couples often fight after having sexual relations with each other. The intimacy and bonding raise the stakes for the issues we have to deal with.

It's good to involve a peacemaker in the confrontation stage, whether it's a pastor or a counselor. A peacemaker can offer the couple three things they badly need at this stage: permission, potency, and protection.[17] Peacemakers can grant permission to both spouses to state their true feelings or grievances without feeling guilty. They can grant the couple the right to state their viewpoints with potency, allowing the negative energy to be dissipated. Finally, they can provide protection for both parties, keeping them from unnecessarily hurting themselves or the other person.

But if that's not done, stage five becomes inevitable.

Stage Five: The Adjustment Phase

The dust settles and the smoke clears. This is the moment of truth for many marriages. Sometimes the adjustment is divorce, adultery, or estrangement, but in a properly managed conflict, the result is a renewed love and commitment to one another.

A counselor is often helpful in this stage as well; in serious confrontations, counselors are almost a necessity. The goal is not to keep peace, but to achieve a lasting peace. Counselors are there to referee or guide the couple into mutually satisfying and agreeable solutions. They can help the husband and wife develop a new set of expectations and commitments to one another. A feeling that "we have been through something together that was tough, but we stuck it out" can enhance the quality and strength of any marriage.

Conclusion

Bill and Lynne Hybels are becoming one of America's best-known couples since he is the pastor of one of the largest congregations in the United States, Willow Creek Community Church. But one Thanksgiving the strain between them reached the breaking point.

Lynne blurted out, "I love you. I just can't handle being married to you. After sixteen years of marriage, I don't know who I am anymore. My life seems lost in yours."

That Thanksgiving confrontation was painful for both of

them. Lynne had sensed it coming for a long time. "I was angry with an anger that had been building for years....It was Thanksgiving and I was not thankful. I was bitter and resentful. I was tired of having to worry about Bill's needs, Bill's desires, Bill's convenience. I was tired of helping him live his life and having no time or energy to live my own."

Following Lynne's explosion, the two sat down at the kitchen table to talk about the past and their marriage. They moved to the couch in the family room. Finally, they sat on the floor against opposite walls. There were tears, there were accusations, but finally there were also answers.

Listen to how Lynne describes the adjustment phase of their Thanksgiving marital turkey shootout:

"We realized that loving doesn't mean we submerge our personhood into someone else's. Making a marriage work doesn't mean we have to give up who we are....I dramatically reduced the pace of my life by learning to say no. I am asking Bill for more help on the home front and receiving enthusiastic response. I am traveling less and liking it more....[We] realized that because we both meant our wedding vows, had a spirit of reconciliation, and were willing to work on conflict resolution, we did not have to panic over disconnection. We were committed to one another."[18]

Of course, the ideal is to avoid reaching the confrontation and adjustment phase by dealing with the problems while they're still small. But we're all human, and sooner or later, we all have to face the painful prospect of working through a major conflict. But conflict doesn't have to destroy a marriage. By choosing collaboration over competition, negotiation, avoidance, or accommodation, a couple can answer Joan River's question, "Can we talk?" by saying, "We sure can."

Chapter Seven

MAKING WAR, NOT LOVE:

Sex and Anger

J im was still smarting from the blowup that had occurred over the weekend. The loud argument over money with his wife, Alissa, had resulted in their not speaking to each other all day Sunday.

Alissa, wanting to be reconciled, came to bed Monday evening in an attractive negligee. She was wearing her best perfume and had put on makeup. "Jim, I love you," she whispered. "I'm sorry for how I acted."

Jim turned his face toward the wall. "I'm tired, Alissa, and I just want to go to sleep." He pulled the covers over his head and didn't say another word.

Alissa, sitting there in her negligee, felt humiliated. She got up and left the room and cried for the next hour. Jim had made his point, but at a terrible cost.

A MATTER OF THE HEART, NOT TECHNIQUE

Starting in the 1970s, the popular market was flooded with books that promised to tell people how to find sexual satisfaction in marriage. Most focused on the right techniques or positions to achieve maximum sexual pleasure. Detailed diagrams of the male and female anatomy accompanied specific instructions on how to stimulate and maintain long episodes of love-making. The authors assumed that only ignorance and poor technique kept couples from achieving a lifetime of nonstop bliss.

But there is no evidence that couples today are achieving more sexual satisfaction in marriage than their parents or grandparents did. Given the high divorce and infidelity rate, it could be argued that people are more unhappy in their marriages than ever before. Studies seem to confirm that conclusion.[1]

While proper techniques can enhance a couple's love life, human sexuality is far more complicated than charts and diagrams of the body. When it comes to building a satisfying sexual relationship in a marriage, it isn't so much a matter of learning the right positions to make love, but learning the right heart attitudes to keep love alive in our relationship. This requires learning the best way to deal with our anger, resentment, and disappointments.

As Donald Joy and others have aptly pointed out, the largest sex organ in the human body is the brain. It's there, above our neck, that the attitudes, emotions, and convictions are formed that ultimately will determine whether we make love or war behind bedroom doors.

HOW TO DESTROY YOUR SEX LIFE

If there is one emotion that prevails in most troubled marriages, it is anger. One or both spouses are angry they married the other person. They are frustrated that they are trapped in a relationship that's become so unhappy. They are impatient with the imperfections and shortcomings of the other person. They are angry that the only options they have are divorce, an affair, or a life of sheer misery.

Besides anger, the other defining emotion in a troubled relationship is fear. Spouses are afraid of getting close, or letting someone get close to them, because they don't feel in love. They fear that life is going to pass them by and that they have blown their only real chance for happiness.

So, where's one of the first places that fear and anger surface in a couple's relationship? In bed. Sex is often the weapon of choice to express such anger because the sexual act requires a vulnerability that encompasses a person's total being. It exposes who you are in virtually every area of your life. To lie naked next to someone is to allow him or her to know you as no one else does. So to reject your husband or wife sexually is to say, as nothing else can say, "I reject you."

Sex is more a thermometer than a thermostat. It reflects the emotional temperature of a relationship rather than alters it. So when anger and fear are present, the mercury drops dramatically. (Is the use of the word *frigid* an accident?) When fear seizes an individual, he or she instinctively withdraws and pushes others away. Sexual desire suffers a case of hypothermia.

As we learned in an earlier chapter, the progression of physical intimacy in the bonding process correlates to what is happening on psychological, social, and spiritual levels as well. When husbands or wives withhold sexual intimacy from each other, they are often saying, "I don't feel bonded to you. I don't want to go through with this act. We're not close to each other. It's a lie."

I've read that prostitutes sometimes refuse to kiss their clients. The reason? It's their method of preserving some remnant of personal integrity. They may be giving their customers access to their body, but they won't give them access to their heart. By denying them a kiss, they are making the statement, "This is only an act; it's not love."

Although there are a variety of reasons to be angry at a spouse—some no doubt legitimate—each is quite costly in the end. If we allow anger to take up permanent residence in our heart, something has gone wrong. When that anger finally destroys our desire for closeness and sexual intimacy, something has gone very wrong.

Jim, whom we met at the beginning of the chapter, didn't realize the true cost of his anger. He thought he could control and punish Alissa by withholding sex. Instead, it only made her more careful to avoid being that vulnerable again.

Sexual blackmail is always a high-stakes game. People using sex in this way usually assume that once they've made their point, or won the argument, their partner will readily resume sexual intercourse with them as if nothing had ever happened. That's a big assumption. People who hold their spouse's sexual needs hostage for several days, weeks, or even months, and then assume everything will return to normal overnight may be in for a surprise. In the case of Alissa, she decided to withhold herself from Jim until he apologized. She wanted to hurt him just as deeply as he had hurt her. They nearly destroyed their marriage because they failed to understand what anger was doing to them.

Perhaps they could have been spared the pain if they had followed some biblical advice. Since God created sex, doesn't it stand to reason that he would know best how human beings can achieve sexual happiness and fulfillment?

Listen to this advice: "The husband should fulfill his marital duty to his wife, and likewise the wife to her husband. The wife's body does not belong to her alone but also to her husband. In the same way, the husband's body does not belong to him alone but also to his wife. Do not deprive each other except by mutual consent and for a time, so that you may devote yourselves to prayer."[2]

What does God say? We should never use sex as a weapon or a means of controlling our partner. It's a violation of the most basic principles of the relationship. We belong to each other; we don't have the right to blackmail or punish our mate by denying his or her needs. It's manipulative, demeaning, and ultimately destructive.

FOUR TECHNIQUES TO DEAL WITH ANGER

So what do we do with our anger in a relationship? As we discussed in the last chapter, the goal is to develop communication skills that will allow us to process that anger. It's not healthy to bury feelings, because when we do, we bury them alive.

That's why we must learn the principle of speaking the truth in love to each other. Some people are naturally blunt and have no problem laying the truth on someone else, but they overlook people's feelings. The results can be devastating.

I was once publicly reprimanded for something I had overlooked. The person was right; I had failed. But the public nature of the rebuke left scars. That conversation should have taken place behind closed doors.

Other people are inclined to show love but have trouble sharing the truth because they don't want to hurt someone else's feelings. The relationship is stymied because they can't bring themselves to share what's really on their heart.

For anger to be drained out of a relationship requires both truth and love. It's what Bill Hybels refers to as "risking chaos to achieve community." We risk confusion, controversy, and even pain in order to achieve reconciliation.

We're not wired to do that naturally. We flinch at the idea of opening up and sharing the hurt we are carrying inside. What if the other person blows up, falls apart, or walks out?

But we must take those risks, in a spirit of love, if we are to deal with our anger. Sometimes we have to disturb the peace, because it's a false peace, if we're going to find lasting meaning and contentment in our relationships.

Hybels, in his thought-provoking book *Honest to God,* suggests the four worst ways to process anger and hide truth in a relationship.[3]

1. Dropping Hints

This approach is used by husbands and wives who don't have the courage to tell someone else their behavior is hurtful or driving them up the wall. They choose instead to drop ever-so-subtle hints.

We all see right through such game playing. The result is usually a worse confrontation than if we had dealt straight in the beginning.

When a couple starts dropping hints about their dissatisfaction with their sexual relationship, it can come out as sarcasm. "How about if I have my needs met first so I can go to sleep and leave you frustrated this time?" Or, "I sure miss the days when you seemed interested in making love, but I guess we all get older, don't we?" Even under the veil of humor, dropping hints can be a disguise for deep-seated animosity. It's not funny, or healthy.

2. Manipulation

This approach is to get people to do what we want by out-maneuvering them. We paint them into a corner where they have no choice but to yield. Perhaps we use sexual or emotional blackmail, or sulk around the house, or pull the covers over our head and turn away when our partner makes a move toward us, as Jim did to Alissa.

We all rebel at being manipulated. We get angry when people try to get us to change without saying what's on their mind or what they need. In the end, it may drive us to the very behavior the other person is trying to change.

3. Guilt tripping

Comedians love to parody the mother who calls her son the night before Mother's Day and says, "No, son, you don't need to take me to lunch tomorrow. After all, who am I? Just your mother. Never mind the fact I was in labor fifty-six hours with you. So what? Forget the fact I gave up the flower of my youth to raise you. Or that I washed floors to put you through college. No, you go out with your wife tomorrow. I'll just go down to the 7-Eleven and buy myself a rose and watch 'Jeopardy.'"

Some marriages operate on the same high-octane guilt. One person has learned the art of making the other person feel so obligated, so indebted that only a grubworm would say no.

Using guilt to control a spouse can destroy the spontaneity and joy of a sexual relationship. "Go ahead, even though I'm not feeling well. I know you have needs." Or, "If you really loved me, you'd cancel your golf game and stay home to make love. But I can't ask you to do that, can I?" Guilt and passion are poor roommates. One or the other eventually has to move out.

4. Intimidation

Perhaps the most dehumanizing alternative to speaking the truth in love is this raw, ugly, crass use of power to get what we want. Shouting, threats, insults, and even violence are pulled out of the drawer to leverage the other person. It destroys the adult-to-adult nature of a marriage and turns it into a parent-to-child relationship.

When I was a fifth grader, my family went camping with a group of professionals from my father's place of employment. A woman in the tent next to us walked over and asked if she could borrow a couple of dollars to buy milk at the camp grocery store. My parents gladly helped her out.

About an hour later shouts erupted from her tent. Then her husband appeared at the door of our trailer and handed the money back to my parents. "She isn't supposed to ask for money," he said, sounding like a father who had just caught his child misbehaving. "She can get all the money she needs from me." The wife was so embarrassed she virtually hid in the tent for the remainder of the weekend. I was not surprised to hear they were divorced a few years later.

Sex can often be used to intimidate a spouse. "If you don't start responding better to me in bed, I may have to start looking elsewhere for my needs to be met." Or, "Don't come near me. If you do, I will move out." When anger takes the form of intimidation, one spouse may get his or her way, but ultimately the marriage is in serious trouble. It's only a matter of time until the meltdown occurs.

IT'S TIME TO RISK CHAOS TO ACHIEVE INTIMACY

If each of these four methods is ineffective in dealing with anger in marriage, what should spouses do? We are back to the only real alternative people have, which is to speak the truth in love.

But that comes hard for many people. If you were raised in a home with fighting, alcoholism, sexual abuse, or other forms of destructive behavior, you learned the one rule that ran the house: Never, ever, speak the truth. Never ever say that dad was a drunk. Never tell anybody what your uncle did to you when you were alone together. Never speak up and say that you hated your parents' fighting.

If you were never given permission to discuss your feelings

or the truth (not at least without paying an enormous price), you just buried them all—alive. As a result, today you may be carrying a mixture of rage, guilt, sadness, low self-esteem, and a fear of intimacy. Such unresolved anger effectively destroys your sex life.

It's time to change. It's time to risk chaos in the context of love. How can we talk about painful things without emotionally stabbing the other person? Hybels offers several positive steps.[4] He suggests that if we're going to share some potentially painful things with our husband or wife, we need to follow some simple guidelines.

Drop Anchor

First, we need to "anchor" our comments by affirming the relationship. "Stacy, my marriage to you means more than anything else in life. I want so much to be sensitive to you and enrich your life. I don't want anything to take away from the relationship we have. That's why I need to talk about our love life and the things that are creating anger and hurt inside me."

Don't Make Accusations

It's vital to make observations instead of accusations. Just because we think something is true, doesn't make it true. Sometimes we can honestly misinterpret situations or behavior and come to an entirely wrong conclusion. We may not understand all that is behind our spouse's behavior or decision.

Accusations hurt, particularly when they're wrong: "You won't make love to me because you're frigid (or impotent)."

Consider how this statement could be rephrased to make an observation, not an accusation: "I sense you're not in the mood for romance tonight. Are you feeling stressed out?"

The dynamics of the situation have changed from a courtroom with prosecuting attorneys to a quiet conversation between friends.

All in Favor Say "I"

Another key element of speaking the truth in love is the use of "I" statements. An "I" statement merely describes your feelings or reactions to another person's behavior. It passes no judgments and makes no pronouncements on the other person's character.

Take the example of Rick and Renée, whose sex life had diminished recently. It had been ten days or more since Rick showed any interest in his wife. One night Renée came to bed and sent the clear signal she wanted romance. But Rick turned on the evening news instead and watched television until he fell asleep.

At breakfast the next morning Renée decided to broach the subject. By using "I" statements she made this a positive encounter: "Rick, darling, I need to talk to you. I'm not certain how to interpret your behavior lately, but let me share how it's impacting me. When you show no sexual interest in me, I feel unwanted, unloved, unattractive. When you choose to watch television rather than make love to me, I feel hurt and humiliated, particularly when I ask you to make love to me. I don't know what you may be dealing with right now, but I'd like to talk about it."

This opened the door for Rick to respond: "Oh, Renée, I'm sorry. I haven't meant to hurt you. I love you and want you just as much as ever. I guess I haven't been the same since I learned they're planning to close our plant next year. I've just been feeling so depressed lately I'm not interested in anything. All my years of service there suddenly seem so worthless. I'm sorry, honey. I guess I never stopped to consider how my behavior might be affecting you."

Renée created a safe environment for discussion by pointing out specific behaviors that were troubling her and by describing their impact on her life. She never accused Rick of anything. She commented only on actions, steering away from character assaults or accusations.

Because Rick was not in the position of defending himself, he was free to share his feelings and to clarify his intentions. That led to the discovery that Rick was probably suffering from mild depression, which often drains the energy from a person's sex drive. Rick was not experiencing negative feelings toward Renée, but rather was having trouble coping with life at the moment. He was grieving over his impending loss of a job, and that grieving took the form of depression.

Their ability to communicate led them to seek help for the real problem—Rick's depression. As a result, they were soon able to resume a life of fulfillment and happiness, treasuring the gift of sexuality they were able to offer each other.

PAROLED FROM PRISONS OF OUR OWN MAKING

It's common in marriage for one partner to desire a sexual relationship, while the other backs off or acts disinterested. Often, anger and fear are the culprits that imprison us and isolate us from each other.

Let me illustrate with this analogy. Several centuries ago Duke Raynald III lived in what is now Belgium. He was grossly overweight, so he was commonly called Crassus, which means "fat." After a violent quarrel, Raynald's younger brother Edward revolted against him and took him prisoner. Edward devised an ingenious plan to hold his brother captive. He had artisans build a room around Raynald in the Nieuwkerk castle, and he promised Raynald he could regain his title and property as soon as he was able to leave the room.

This would not have been difficult for most people since the room had several windows and a door, none of which were locked or barred. The problem was Raynald's size. To go through the door and regain his freedom, he needed to lose weight. But Edward knew his older brother was captive to his appetites, and each day he sent Raynald a variety of delicious foods. Instead of losing weight and gaining his freedom, Raynald grew fatter.

When Duke Edward was accused of cruelty, he had a ready answer. "My brother is not a prisoner. He may leave when he so wills."[5]

What does a story like this have to do with a couple's frustrating sex life? Simply this. When we feed our anger and fear or our appetite for revenge, we confine ourselves to a dungeon of our own making. The irony is this. We can find freedom and happiness in our sexual relationship just as soon as we choose to deal with anger in a positive way. If we don't, we may eventually start sleeping in other parts of the house, or with someone else. We end up making war, not love.

Is there a way to restore passion in a marriage where the fire seems nearly extinguished? Can couples renew their love life? Definitely. In the next chapter we'll discover the true aphrodisiacs of marriage, the mysterious elements that can bring heat and intensity back to a cold and apathetic sexual relationship. Chances are you haven't read about them in supermarket tabloids or heard them discussed on a prime time talk show. But the formula is as old as marriage itself.

Chapter Eight

THREE TRUE APHRODISIACS

The commercials for perfumes and colognes are all pretty much the same. A man splashes on his musk-scented aftershave, walks out into public, and gorgeous models suddenly appear from every direction with desire burning in their eyes. A woman uses an expensive New York perfume, and suddenly she's transported to a Greek isle where rugged and attractive men follow her down the beach.

What the purveyors of modern Madison Avenue scents are doing is as old as romance itself. They're trying to sell you and me on the notion that their potion can instantly create sexual desire in another person. They hope to convince us they've discovered a modern aphrodisiac.

LEAH'S LOVE POTION

Is there such a thing as a love potion? Throughout history cultures have believed that certain plants or foods could heighten and intensify sexual passion, making a person irresistible to others. Believe it or not, that was even the case in the days of Jacob and Leah. After several years of being married to her reluctant husband, Leah pursued a desperate strategy to gain Jacob's love and affection. Anyone who accuses the Scriptures of lacking candor in describing human relationships or sexuality needs to reread this story:

> During the wheat harvest, Reuben [Jacob and Leah's oldest son] went out into the fields and found some mandrake plants, which he brought to his mother Leah. Rachel said to Leah, "Please give me some of your son's mandrakes."
>
> But she said to her, "Wasn't it enough that you took away my husband? Will you take my son's mandrakes too?"
>
> "Very well," Rachel said, "he can sleep with you tonight in return for your son's mandrakes."
>
> So when Jacob came in from the fields that evening, Leah went out to meet him. "You must sleep with me," she said. "I have hired you with my son's mandrakes." So he slept with her that night.[1]

The story illustrates the pain and heartache that a troubled sex life can bring to marriage. It was perhaps common knowledge that Jacob and Leah's marriage was in trouble. The fact that it had been years since the birth of their last child was a clue. Since Jacob's only interest in Leah appeared to be her ability to bear children, and since she had been infertile, we may assume Jacob now stayed away from her entirely.

Reuben was out in the fields during the harvest season when he discovered mandrakes growing in the wild. According to scholars, in ancient cultures mandrakes were believed to be aphrodisiacs and were highly prized (for obvious reasons).

Reuben ran home to show his mother his precious find. While it's a matter of pure speculation, he might have said something like, "Mother, look what I've found. Mandrakes. Please take them." Respect probably kept him from saying the obvious, but in his heart he must have been thinking, *These ought to get Dad interested in you again.*

Word of Reuben's exotic find apparently spread quickly through the camp. Rachel, perhaps alarmed by the implications of Leah's possessing the mysterious love plant, rushed over and begged for a few samples of the aphrodisiac for herself.

The true state of Jacob and Leah's nonexistent sexual relationship is now confirmed. Listen to the pain in Leah's voice, "Wasn't it enough that you took away my husband? Will you take my son's mandrakes too?" A paraphrase of Leah's words might be, "Rachel, isn't it enough that Jacob sleeps only with you? Do you know how long it's been since I've experienced his tenderness, his touch, his embrace? Do you know how many nights I've watched him enter your tent while he walked past mine? Now that I've found something to offer me the slim hope that he might make love to me again and I might bear him another child, you want to steal that from me, too? Have you no shame, Rachel?"

Rachel, perhaps convicted by the truth of Leah's words or perhaps sensing she had lost control of the situation, decided to strike a bargain. She didn't want to leave the mandrakes in Leah's hands, fearing they might effectively arouse Jacob's passion and allow Leah to steal him away from her. So Rachel proposed a compromise. If Leah would turn over the mandrakes, she could have Jacob for one night.

Maybe Rachel was thinking, *What's only one night? Besides, after tonight, I'll be the one with the mandrakes, and Jacob won't be able to stay away from me.*

If there is any lingering doubt about Jacob and Leah's sex

life, listen to their discussion in the field. Jacob was returning from the day's work, tired and exhausted, when Leah ran out to meet him. She informed the surprised Jacob that she had purchased him for a one-night stand. "'You must sleep with me,' she said. 'I have hired you with my son's mandrakes.' So he slept with her that night." Jacob offered no protest over the deal, perhaps aroused by the news that Rachel had the love plant in her possession.

Can you imagine a marriage that has deteriorated to the point where one spouse has to hire the other for the night? That's exactly where Leah stood with Jacob.

Unfortunately, in many marriages that have gotten offtrack, one partner couldn't even pay the other to make love. Oh, they may go through the act every once in a while, but without genuine tenderness or desire. It's more a duty or a matter of routine than an act of true marriage. As in the case of Leah, one partner becomes desperate to win back the affection and passion of the other.

ARTIFICIAL APHRODISIACS

While it's doubtful that mandrakes were actual aphrodisiacs, partners in unhappy marriages often are willing to try any artificial means to capture the sexual attention of their disinterested partner.

Sex on Paper

The most common form of mandrake today is pornography. Couples turn to *Playboy* magazines, R-rated or NC-17 videos, or other hard-core materials to arouse passion in their marriage. I'm stunned by the number of couples who admit to allowing their partner to use pornographic magazines or literature during sexual intercourse to increase the sizzle in their love life. Its negative impact on people's attitudes toward marriage is well documented.[2] It's a great error for several reasons.

First, it won't lead to a sustained love life. Pornography is an addictive habit of diminishing returns. It requires greater and greater doses to achieve the same result, which means that using pictures and videos to turn on your partner will eventually give out. It can't sustain its sizzle.

I remember an advertisement in a popular weekly magazine that showed a couple sitting in front of a television, holding shot glasses of whisky and watching a sexy video. It was intended to titillate the consumer into believing that whiskey and erotic videos combine to create the ultimate lovemaking experience. The truth is, it may work at first. But over time more bottles of whisky and sexier videos are required to achieve the same effect.

Which leads to the second problem. Inevitably, the use of pornography in lovemaking leads to more sordid and aberrant materials. As the graphic nature of the pornographic literature increases, it becomes more bizarre and abnormal, drawing couples further away from normal sexual activity.

Finally, the use of pornography in the bedroom is essentially sex with someone else. At best, it's sexual fantasizing about another person. At worst, it's visual adultery. It feeds lust for a person you've never met, desire for an individual you'll never have a genuine relationship with, and hunger for someone you have no commitment to, or they to you. It's sex on paper.

As we've discussed in earlier chapters, the bonding process is intended to progress between two real human beings who actually see, talk to, and touch each other. Sex with the aid of pornography, whether magazines or videos, transfers that highly intense emotional and psychological attachment to someone other than your spouse. The result is a distancing and detachment from your own life's partner. It's as if you're making love to two different people at the same time. You've allowed another lover to enter the bedroom. That's as destructive to true intimacy as anything I can think of.

Perhaps the most famous article in the history of *Leadership Journal* was a minister's account of his private struggle with lust. He admitted that he started down the road toward pornography addiction the weekend he visited a bar with nude dancers. For the next several years his life was a nightmare of increasingly compulsive and obsessive behaviors that nearly destroyed his marriage and career.

In desperation, he sought the counsel of an older and respected pastor. As he poured out his secret pain, the older pastor stared at him, then began blinking back tears, and eventually broke into sobs. The older man handed the younger one several prescriptions he was taking to treat his own venereal diseases. The older minister confessed to decades of immoral behavior, which began with using pornography earlier in his life. It had cost him everything worthwhile.

Fortunately, the story has a redemptive ending. The younger pastor was so frightened by the prospect of ending up like the older pastor that he resolved to find help and give up his addiction. The article ends with the pastor saying that once he found freedom from his habit his marriage changed dramatically. His sexual relationship with his wife took on a new beauty and meaning he had never known. He felt purity and love energize their relationship, rather than the insatiable and demanding obsessions that pornography had created in his life.[3]

Getting High

Drugs and alcohol are two other artificial aphrodisiacs that some couples use to try to stimulate a disappointing love life.

The myth is that sex is best while you're drunk or high. But it's just that—a myth.

If a couple is resorting to chemical substances in order to enjoy each other, the clock is already ticking on the eventual destruction of their relationship. Drugs can no more build intimacy or satisfaction in a relationship than they can help any of us face life's problems more effectively. They may anesthetize our emotional pain, or allow us a few minutes of relief from our inhibitions, but overall the addictive nature of drugs ensures that they will steal more happiness from us than they will ever be able to offer. Just ask the husband or wife of an alcoholic how much better booze makes their sex life. My counseling experience suggests that many men who are alcoholics struggle with impotency. Sobriety is their only hope for regaining the ability to be intimate with their wives.

Sexual happiness in marriage can't be purchased at the mall, rolled and smoked behind closed doors, or bought in the back room of an adult bookstore. These "aphrodisiacs" miss the point of true sexual intimacy, because it really is a matter of the heart.

THE TRUE APHRODISIACS

That's the good news. Young or old, rich or poor, handsome or homely, every married individual can possess the true love stimulants of marriage.

What are these mysterious formulas for heightening and sustaining sexual enjoyment in marriage? They may surprise you. They are forgiveness, surrender, and unselfishness. More than anything else I know, they can restore pleasure and fulfillment to a couple's sex life. They are the true aphrodisiacs, found not in bottles, mysterious plants, or rain forests, but in the souls of a man and woman. Generous doses of each one, taken regularly, can rejuvenate a sexual relationship.

The Magnetism of Forgiveness

Forgiveness—an aphrodisiac that's available in all parts of the world, but rarely used. When it is used, it can dramatically alter the chemistry between two people. As we discussed in the last chapter, the negative emotions of anger and fear can destroy the sexual relationship between a husband and wife. If we're seething with bitterness toward our mate, there's little or no chance we'll seek out or accept sexual intimacy.

I watched a talk show one afternoon that featured couples who had decided to get a divorce. When one husband was asked if it bothered him that his estranged wife had taken a lover, he replied, "I don't care what she does. In fact, I hope she's run over by a train one of these days so I can get her out of my life." Imagine, he wanted her dead.

But if anger can drive a couple that far apart, forgiveness can have just the opposite effect. It can be positively magnetic. Think back on the worst fights you and your spouse have ever had. Were you able to resolve those arguments, perhaps with tears, by offering and receiving genuine forgiveness? Do you remember where that led? Chances are, you soon were enjoying the best sex you had experienced in a long time. The old adage is true, "The best part of fighting is making up."

Why this sudden burst of sexual attraction when a couple resolves a fight and reconciles? It's simple. Our essential oneness has been restored, and we want to express that in a physical way. A depth of intimacy has just been achieved. We feel more under-stood, more appreciated, more accepted for who we are, and that ignites the main engines of sexual desire and fuels passion with white hot intensity.

But granting forgiveness is not always easy. How do we for-give a person we don't feel like forgiving? Or someone who hasn't asked for our forgiveness? It's not easy, I'll grant you. If it were, more couples would choose that route rather than divorce court.

Forgiveness is essentially a choice we make, not a feeling we achieve. It requires, by an act of our will, releasing other people from the moral debt they owe us. Forgiveness is not given because it's earned or deserved but because it's needed. Forgiveness is mercy, not justice.

The story is told of a soldier during the Revolutionary War who had deserted the ranks and was later captured. He was tried and sentenced to die. The order was about to be carried out when a Methodist circuit-riding preacher by the name of Peter Miller rode breathless into the camp.

"I must see General Washington," he said. He was ushered into the general's tent. There he explained that he had ridden for an entire day to ask for a pardon for the condemned soldier.

"Is he a friend of yours?" Washington asked.

"No, he is one of my worst enemies," the preacher replied.

"You rode for an entire day to ask for a pardon for your worst enemy? Why?"

"Because he needs it," Miller replied.

Washington was so moved by Miller's act of grace that he granted the pardon. That's precisely the point of forgiveness. We offer it because it's needed, not because it's deserved.

What makes forgiveness difficult is our innate desire for justice. Something within us demands that punishment be paid for a wrong we've experienced.

"I will forgive my wife when she finally admits she's been wrong all these years."

"I won't forgive Bill until he quits making thoughtless remarks about me."

"He can't just say 'I'm sorry' and think that makes everything all right."

If necessary, we can dredge up enough from the past to justify a lifetime of grudges. We can rationalize a thousand and one reasons to be vindictive. And if we refuse to forgive until the other person has paid his debt to us, when is the payment sufficient? When has the other person suffered enough? How much pain does he or she deserve? When is it time to grant release?

If we don't offer forgiveness, then we, like the obese Raynald III, become lifetime prisoners of our making. We stay bound by our own bitterness, acrimony, and resentment.

After the Civil War had ended, General Robert E. Lee was visiting in the home of a woman whose property had been pillaged by the invading Union army. A once beautiful oak tree now stood gnarled and disfigured in the front yard.

"What should I do, General?" the woman asked, her face etched with anger and a desire for revenge.

"Madam, I would advise you to cut it down and forget about it," he calmly replied. The general had learned not only to command armies but his emotions as well—often a far more difficult task.

Forgiveness occurs when we choose to override our desire for punishment and payment and we release our husband or wife from any further moral debt to us. It may come with difficulty, it may come slowly, it may even come in stages, but if it is our desire to forgive, it will occur.

The resources of God can be of such help here. He is by nature forgiving, and he offers us the strength and ability to forgive our mate when everything within us screams, "No! No! I can never forgive what has been done to me." Even couples who have endured the nightmare of adultery, or who have discovered painful things about each other's past, have found that forgiveness can heal their relationship. The memories, the hurt, and the scars may endure, but forgiveness allows the marriage to go forward.

After they were married, Jim learned that Anita had been intimate with other men when she was single. It took him weeks of dealing with his anger, hurt, and disappointment before he could show affection toward her again. Part of him wanted to forgive her; the other part wanted to punish her for her earlier immorality. Eventually Jim realized that Anita could not change her past, even if she wanted to. The only thing that could be changed was his attitude toward her past. So, with God's help, he chose to forgive her, and he told her so. He decided to focus on his love for her and her faithfulness to him throughout their married life. His willingness to forgive rekindled the intimacy in their marriage, allowing them both to go on with their lives and leave the past behind. What a shame if a lack of forgiveness had been allowed to destroy a truly beautiful relationship.

The Triumph of Surrender

Surrender is the second enduring, emotional aphrodisiac that can enhance a couple's sex life.

All of us bring fears, inhibitions, and insecurities to our marriage, which will surface in our sexual relationship. The level of intimacy and vulnerability that the Creator designed into the sex act forces these hidden fears to the surface.

Tammy was raised in an emotionally distant home. Her parents insisted that she be perfect at everything she did, and with a sweet face and natural talents, she seemed to meet their every expectation. But over time her view of love became distorted. She believed that her parents' love and acceptance were based on her being the perfect daughter. Part of that perfect daughter image was shaped by the subtle message that sex was dirty and nice girls should have no interest in it. Tammy confused the truth that sex outside of marriage is wrong with the idea that her sexual nature itself was wrong.

To her credit, she remained a virgin throughout her teenage years and into young adulthood. After college she met a fine young man whom she fell in love with and planned to marry. Little did Tammy know it, but she was headed for real problems in her relationship with her husband. Years of associating acceptance and love with a denial of her own sexuality had set her up for a trauma.

It happened on the honeymoon. When she and her new husband reached the bridal suite, she broke out in hives. In her mind, engaging in sexual intercourse would completely destroy her perfect daughter image, the basis for her self-identity growing up. Sexual intercourse would sully her, leaving her a "less than perfect" person, or so her distorted conscience told her.

She wanted to be intimate with her husband, but she couldn't get past the feeling she was doing something wrong. Her feelings that sex was disgusting, even dirty, were simply overwhelming, and her skin betrayed the anguish inside.

But an understanding of surrender in marriage can heal even someone like Tammy. God never designed anything that was disgusting, dirty, or sinful. Sexuality is among his highest gifts to humanity. In the context of marriage the sexual act is pure, life giving, even holy in his sight. But it requires surrender in order to be enjoyed to its fullest.

What is surrender in marriage? It's essentially giving our life away in order to get it back again. It is in no sense giving up our right to be an individual, or becoming the slave of another, or eradicating our personhood, dignity, or uniqueness. Surrender is voluntarily yielding ourselves to another in love. It is letting go of the fears and inhibitions that create barriers between two people whom God designed to "become one flesh."

Let's suppose a building is on fire. On the third floor balcony a terrified tenant hangs on to the railing with a death grip. As a fireman climbs the ladder and reaches him, he urges the man to let go of the railing so he may be carried to safety. The flames are roaring, smoke is billowing, and the person is scared to death. He can choose either to hang on and lose his life, or let go and get it back again. That's surrender. In the same fashion, when we let go of our fears and apprehensions and choose to trust another human being in the act of sexual intimacy, we haven't lost who we are. We've surrendered ourselves to our partner's love and care and have found a new dimension of human happiness.

That's the paradox of life. When we give up, we gain back. When we yield, we overcome. When we sacrifice, we are enriched.

Real surrender in marriage is not one-sided. A biblical view of sex calls for mutual submission. Remember the apostle's words: "The wife's body does not belong to her alone but also to her husband. In the same way, the husband's body does not belong to him alone but also to his wife."[4] The apostle says surrender is reciprocal, mutual, two-sided.

Tammy had the mistaken notion that she had lost something when she engaged in intercourse with her husband. Not at all. In surrendering her body to her husband, and he doing likewise, they both gained the union and "one flesh" that the Creator designed to give us maximum fulfillment and joy in marriage.

What Tammy needed to lose was her false sense of guilt and shame. Her upbringing of perfectionism and conditional love had left her feeling sinful for enjoying the intimacy God designed for marriage. She needed to surrender her false ideas that her sexuality was a curse, not a blessing. She also needed to realize that God values us, not because we earn it, but because he loves us just as we are.

The Dividends of Unselfishness

The final aphrodisiac—and perhaps the most elusive—is unselfishness.

"I'm sick of it!" Martha said as she slammed the dishes in the sink. "I'm just fed up with Joe taking every day of our vacation to go fishing. He never stops and asks what I'd like to do."

Although I was only a teenager at the time, I recall seeing the anger in the face of my friend's mom. Joe, obviously insensitive or unconcerned about his wife's feelings, was dragging her out into a boat for two weeks, and she didn't want to go. This wasn't going to be a second honeymoon. Joe seemed more infatuated with northern pike and walleye than with his wife.

Men can easily become self-centered, particularly when it comes to sexuality. The nature of males' sexual functioning predisposes us to quick arousal and quick satisfaction. Women, on the other hand, sometimes take far longer to become sexually excited and usually longer to be satisfied. It's the difference between a dragster and a freight train. Drag cars roar to life, squeal off the starting line, and, before you know it, put on the brakes. Freight trains, on the other hand, take a long time to get rolling. But once they do, they're hard to stop.

If wives have one persistent complaint about their husband's sexual performance, it is that they rush things. Husbands become so preoccupied with satisfying their own needs, due to their quick arousal, they forget to bring their mate along with them. While it may be natural for men, it is also quite selfish.

"As soon as my husband is finished, he goes to sleep" is a common complaint among women. It's a clear signal that the husband has not taken time to bring his wife along with him, nor stayed around to ensure that she has experienced climax as well.

Good sex begins with a consideration for our mate's needs, not our own. We should not deny each other a sexual relationship, or act bored or disinterested in the middle of the act.

I once counseled a couple, both recovering alcoholics, who were having serious marriage problems. When I had a chance to sit down with them, the wife began ridiculing her husband's sexual performance. "I can't tell you how many times it's ended just as soon as it got started," she said as she lit a cigarette. "He says, 'whoops,' and it's all over." She blew smoke in his direction. I looked over at him and saw him slink down in his chair, humiliated. What she said may have been true, but her sarcastic tone and smirk sent the loud and clear message she considered him a failure. I suspected the real problem in their sexual relationship was not his premature ejaculations, but her predominant disrespect for him. The two were probably related.

Some experts suggest women experience their sexual arousal more on a psycho-social-physiological level. It is the tenderness and communication in the relationship that excite women. Perhaps the best technique for helping a woman achieve climax in the sexual act is to show her tenderness and talk to her, stimulating her mind and imagination. That's why love, sensitivity, and romance are so important to meeting the sexual needs of a woman.

Women tend to buy more romance novels than men do. It's not because they contain steamy and prurient scenes (although many do), but because they focus on romance and relationships. That's a deeply felt need in the female soul. Husbands who fail to romance their wives throughout the day often find a disinterested or disappointed mate awaiting them when they finally slip into bed at night. It's a little late to start showing a real interest in communication and tenderness (although it's worth a try).

Men, on the other hand, operate far more on a biological-visual-hydraulic level. Simply seeing a woman is enough to provide sexual arousal (all the fashion designers understand this). Whether or not a word is exchanged all day between the two, the husband can be ready for action at a moment's notice.

Unselfishness can help restore passion to a couple's love life. As spouses, we must listen to each other, talk together, and show one another sensitivity and tenderness. We must communicate to our mates that they are attractive and important to us.

Once we move into the bedroom, we need to take things slow. We need to hug and hold our spouse in a caring and intimate manner, not simply for sexual stimulation. Fortunately, it doesn't have to be an either/or choice. We need to take the time to say, "You are cherished and loved."

I still recall sitting in the office of a pastor one day when his wife pulled up in front of the church. "Excuse me, Bob," he said. "I must go make love to my wife." Single at the time, I was left speechless as he disappeared out the door and climbed into the front seat of his wife's car. He did go make love to her, but not in the popular sense of the term. For nearly thirty minutes he sat next to her in the front seat, hugging and cuddling her. I stood at the window, shaking my head in disbelief.

He taught me a valuable lesson that day: Making love to your wife begins long before you close the bedroom door.

Husbands need to take the time to ensure their wives experience sexual release and fulfillment. Far too many men simply turn over and start snoring once they've been satisfied. That's selfishness in its purest sense. Experts also tell us that most women are capable of achieving multiple climaxes during intercourse. It's the sensitive and giving husband who makes sure her needs are satisfied before his.

If you have specific questions in this area, I suggest you discuss the matter with a counselor or your personal physician. He or she can help explain the proper methods of ensuring both partners experience the joy and pleasure God designed into this sacred, mysterious, and bonding experience. There are numerous helpful books on the subject as well, such as *Intended for Pleasure* by Dr. Ed Wheat or *The Act of Marriage* by Tim and Beverly LaHaye.

Unselfishness which builds intimacy extends beyond the bedroom. It ought to be a way of life. I suggest couples do three things each day, even if they don't feel like it.

First, hug each other for at least ninety seconds. It may feel awkward at first, but the payoffs are enormous. Real and important transactions take place in a relationship when we hold each other in our arms for an extended time.

Second, I suggest couples call one another at least twice during the day. It allows you to stay in touch, to remain connected, so that all your distracting business doesn't have to be handled when you get home at night.

Finally, I suggest you ask each other, "What do you need from me at this very moment?" That type of unselfish question can do much to help a burdened or overworked person find love and comfort in a relationship. When our spouses need time alone, we need to gather up the kids and offer them the gift of silence and tranquility. When our mates need someone to talk to, we need to put down the paper or the book, look them in the eye, and listen. When they just need to be held, we need to hold them and assure them of how much we love them.

All of these unselfish acts are cumulative in a marriage. Over time they actually cause us to love our spouse more. The more unselfishly we treat someone, the more highly we value them. The more highly we value them, the more we love them. It's a delicious—not vicious—cycle that leads upward.

The Value of Respect

Another powerful come-on is to show our spouse respect. We all crave respect and admiration, and they ignite passion. On the other hand, one of the best ways to destroy sexual interest is to show disrespect for our mate.

"If I don't keep reminding Roger to speak up at gatherings, he'll never make any friends."

"Kim, that's an ugly blouse. You need to ask me before you wear something like that."

"David, when are you going to fix this sink? This is the fourth time I've had to ask you. Other husbands take care of things like this without even having to be asked."

Remember the poll of the four hundred divorced men? Their number one criterion for the next person they married was some-one who treated them as if they were "best friends." Best friends don't put each other down in public, share embarrassing facts about each other on the telephone, or criticize each other at home.

Funny thing about respect. The more we offer it to some-one, the more we enjoy being with that person. The less respect we show, the less often we care to spend time together.

None of us should dare to assume the role of re-Creator in someone else's life. If God made some people quiet, shy, and reflective, we have no business trying to turn them into extro-verts that enjoy wearing a letter sweater and inviting shoppers into a Disney store. If God made others artsy, creative, and spon-taneous, it's pure presumption to try to transform them into technical, detail-oriented, engineer types.

Nine times out of ten we try to remake people in our own image. That's a mistake. To begin with, we're flawed goods, too. If they don't have the same temperament, emotional makeup, and talents we do, it's futile to spend years trying to reshape their basic personality structure. We might make them nervous and unhappy, but we'll never change who they truly are.

The truth is we don't have to be exactly alike to love and respect each other. Nor is it my personal responsibility to spend a lifetime retooling my mate. My time and energy would be much better spent reworking who I am so that I will get along better with the other person.

For Appearance' Sake

One final word of caution to wives and husbands both. Don't let your appearance go simply because you're married and the courting game is over. Husbands aren't expecting "the total woman" to meet them at the door dressed in Saran Wrap. (Joan Rivers claims she tried it once and her husband replied, "What? Leftovers again?") Men simply want their wives to look as if they are meeting someone important—their husbands. Wives aren't expecting Tom Cruise or Kevin Costner look-alikes, but they do appreciate men who watch their weight and keep themselves in good shape.

Of course, age will eventually change the bodies of both men and women. And when we're bald, stooped over, or gray, the deeper work of love and respect will pay its dividends. We will still feel attraction for each other, not based on outward appearances but on the bonding that has occurred in our souls.

One of our dear friends is a lady ninety-two years old. She and her husband were married over fifty years. They survived both world wars, the depression, the cold war, and all the other tumultuous events of the century before he died at the age of eighty-six. Her husband's picture still hangs in her bedroom, and when she speaks of him, the respect in her voice conveys that she truly loved him. His last picture shows a tired man with drawn eyes. But to her, he left this world the most attractive man she had ever met.

Conclusion

Obsession. Taboo. Musk. You've heard the names and seen the commercials. They are the modern mandrakes, the aphrodisiacs that promise compulsive attraction between the sexes. But in the end, they are just a seventy-five-dollar-an-ounce disappointment. The human personality structure is simply too complicated to be controlled by exotic fragrances. True sexual attraction and fulfillment in marriage are the result of our character, not our cologne. Forgiveness, surrender, and unselfishness—when offered in love and sincerity—are the elements of irresistible love.

WAS IT ALL A MISTAKE?

The Higher and Hidden Purposes of God

Truman Robertson, a good friend of mine, is the founder and former director of Fort Wilderness, a beautiful camp in the north woods of Wisconsin. One summer day he asked two boys to go burn the camp garbage. The two eager campers readily agreed and headed off to the garbage pit. Once they got there, they hit on a plan to take care of the job faster and more efficiently.

They found a five-gallon container of high-octane fuel and decided to soak the garbage before lighting the match. They were about to set the rubbish ablaze when they decided it might be wise to put some distance between the bonfire and themselves.

Then they hit upon another ingenious plan. They took a bow and arrow, tied a rag on the end of the arrow, and lit it just as they had seen in a Western. Taking careful aim, they let it fly. The projectile followed a perfect arc into the center of the pit.

The ensuing explosion was heard for several miles. Onlookers claim to have seen soup cans, corncobs, and milk cartons fly at least fifty feet into the sky. Garbage literally rained down on the camp like leftovers from heaven.

The two boys, hunched behind a rock, were nearly deafened by the blast. When they cautiously emerged to survey the devastation, they were speechless. Garbage hung from the trees. Debris was scattered in every direction. All that was left of the garbage pit was a crater approximately twenty feet deep.

It had all seemed like such a good idea. But the best that could be said of the entire incident was that no one had been killed.

The same is true of many marriages. They start out as such a good idea. The engagement, the wedding, the new life together. But when the marital explosions hit and people are left dazed, covered with emotional debris, and staring into a gaping pit of despair and unhappiness, they are tempted to stop and ask, "Was this all a big mistake?"

Every time I meet people who are going through a divorce, or who have fallen into adultery, or who simply hate being married, I'm reminded that they didn't have this in mind that beautiful Saturday afternoon in June. As they dressed in elegant clothes and recited solemn vows, surrounded by friends and family, they never dreamed it would turn out like this. They think, "I wasn't supposed to hate her as much as I do." "I wasn't supposed to get this sick feeling in my stomach when I hear him come home at night." "I wasn't supposed to end up dreading each family get-together where I have to pretend everything is all right when it isn't."

When people reach the conclusion that their marriage never should have been, the next logical question is "Then why go on? It's stupid. This obviously wasn't the right thing to do, so why don't I just end it?"

BUT WHAT DOES GOD THINK?

That's where I would like to interrupt their train of thought and challenge them with this question, "Who says that it's all a big mistake?" On what authority can you or I announce that our marriage never should have been? Because our feelings tell us so? Or because our parents think our mate is a loser? Or because a counselor has told us we need to leave the marriage to find ourselves? Before we-pack our bags or call the lawyer, we need to consider this question: "Does God think my marriage was a big mistake?"

"What do you mean what does God think?" someone might protest. "How in the world am I supposed to know the mind of God anyway? All I know is that I'm terribly unhappy and a loving God could never want anyone to feel as bad as I do."

I agree that God doesn't enjoy seeing you suffer emotional pain and sorrow. His heart hurts when yours does. But that doesn't mean that your marriage is a big mistake. All it means is that you are unhappy and at the moment you feel your marriage is a big mistake.

ANYTHING OF VALUE
IS WORTH SUFFERING FOR

Let's imagine for a moment that you and I had an opportunity to talk about your marriage at a time when you were fed up and wanting out.

"Bob, my marriage is a disaster. It's the biggest regret of my life. I should have never married the person I did."

My response might be, "I hear your pain, your unhappiness, and your desire to see something change in your marriage. But I'm not convinced that your marriage is a big mistake."

"Why not? How could I be this unhappy and possibly be married to the right person?"

"Let me answer that with another question. Was going through college worthwhile?"

"Of course it was."

"Did you ever want to quit, particularly during finals week?"

"Sure. I got so tired and worn out I wanted to drop out and never look back. I hated school during those moments."

"Let me ask you another question" (assuming I'm now talking to a woman). "When you had your first child and you were in the midst of hard labor, did you ever wish you had not decided to get pregnant in the first place?"

"Are you kidding? You men will never understand just how painful labor can get."

"But was it worth the agony?"

"Of course. I love my child. I wouldn't trade her for anything in the world."

"Then can you agree that even though you endured great suffering, what you gained from the experience offset the sacrifices involved?"

"Yes."

"If you can accept that, then let me suggest the pain you're experiencing today is not iron-clad evidence you married the wrong person. Pain can only tell you that something is wrong and needs to be addressed in your relationship. That's quite different from saying your marriage is a big mistake."

Ask people who have labored, fought, cried, hurt, but persevered in a worthwhile task, and they will tell you it's become a valuable, if not the most valuable, experience of their entire life. Sigmund Freud said, "Someday, given enough time, we will look back on our lives and discover the most difficult moments have become the most precious to us."

I try to tell my children what it was like to grow up in the sixties. My high school was shut down by a student protest. My uncle was killed in Vietnam. A president was shot when I was in third grade. Neighbors were angry at us because we welcomed a black man and his white wife into our home. My sister's university transcripts were burned in a campus protest. Students brought "magic brownies" laced with marijuana to my school and got high during lunch. I went to summer school in Washington, D.C., where I encountered radicals who claimed they were there to overthrow the government.

When I try to describe that era to my young children, they just look at me with bewilderment. Strange as it may sound, I now value those years. Painful as they were, the fact that I survived them has been a source of strength and even purpose in my life.

In the same way, it may seem pointless today to endure the pain and hardship of a marriage that started off wrong. And if we project our feelings out another five, ten, or fifty years, staying in the marriage seems too much to ask. No one can or should live with that much unhappiness we tell ourselves.

But just as the tumultuous sixties eventually passed on, so a difficult season in a marriage can give way to a much more fulfilling and joyful experience. Ask a couple who has made it to the half-century mark, and they'll no doubt tell you about some grim years along the way—the time he lost his job, or one of their children died at birth, or a close family member was struck down with a disease. But if you watch closely, particularly the way they look into each other's eyes, you'll probably catch a glimpse of the deep understanding that exists between them. They will quietly acknowledge to each other, "We went through that together, and we survived it. I thank God that I had you to go through it with me."

Let me assure you, I'm no advocate of masochism. I don't believe in suffering for the sake of suffering, nor do I gain any pleasure from it. But I do believe in the redemptive value of our pain if we use it to our advantage. If we make it serve us, if we allow it to do its good work in our lives, if we use it to motivate us to take action, then it can become something positive.

It all comes back to believing there is an authority higher than our emotions, our immediate circumstances, or the opinion of others. It goes back to believing that God may have a higher and unseen purpose in our marriage than we realize at the moment. Trusting that he is working out a plan for our lives can make all the difference.

LESSONS FROM LEAH

Let's go back to Jacob and Leah. Leah is, by my standards, a remarkable woman. If *Time* magazine had been in existence almost four thousand years ago, she would have been my nomination for Person of the Year.

If any woman on earth at the time had the right to say, "God? What God?" it was Leah. She had virtually no rights as a female member of an ancient tribal society. She was used by her father to cheat Jacob out of another seven years of free labor. And Jacob hardly treated her as a wife. Yet she refused to surrender her faith that God was demonstrating his love and concern for her. That's evident from the names she gave her sons. Each one was an acknowledgment that God was quietly, if not mysteriously, involved in the events of her life.

When Reuben was born, she said, "*It is because the Lord has seen* my misery." When Simeon entered the world, she confessed, "*Because the Lord heard* that I am not loved, he gave me this one too." The same was true at the birth of Issachar: "*God has rewarded me.*" And Zebulun: "*God has presented me* with a precious gift."[1] When each of her six sons was born, Leah claimed it was proof that God had not forgotten her but was showering her with his mercy and affection.

Her faith continued strong in spite of the fact that Jacob kept treating her like a second-class citizen. Although Leah hoped that her sons would change his heart, there is little evidence that he softened toward her at this stage in his life. Nonetheless, she continued to believe and worship God.

Anyone who is struggling with a disappointing or "unbearable" marriage can take great encouragement from the example of Leah. Her life is proof that outward circumstances are not always an indication of God's concern and compassion for us. Just because our marriage is hurting doesn't mean God no longer loves us. He may be using this particularly agonizing period in our life to communicate with us.

The great Oxford scholar C. S. Lewis once wrote, "Pain is God's megaphone." It does get our attention. It does drive us from our self-sufficiency to seek the help and strength that God longs to offer us. Lewis wrote from his own experience. A confirmed bachelor for most of his life, he eventually married a woman who was suffering from cancer. By most accounts, he did it more out of duty than love.

But in the few years they were married, he learned to love Joy deeply. By the time she died, she had become the most precious person on earth to him. In his book *A Grief Observed* Lewis shares his heart-rending experience of losing the person he had learned to love more than his own life.

Which brings us back to Leah. The worse things were with Jacob, the more real God seemed to her. Was she in denial? Was her faith in God just a spiritual fix to get her through another tough week with a loveless husband and a jealous sister? Was the "God talk" just a crutch? Or was God truly the strength of her life?

The answer lies in the birth of her fourth son, Judah. In that event God honored Leah's confidence that he was working in her life in some mysterious and wonderful fashion. When Leah's fourth son was born, she said, "'This time I will praise the Lord.' So she named him Judah." Scholars note that the name Judah sounds like and is probably derived from the Hebrew word for "praise."[2]

You may still be asking, "But how does naming a child 'Judah' prove that Leah's faith was real? How does that prove God was working behind the scenes in her life and marriage to accomplish a higher and hidden purpose?"

LEAH IN THE PLAN OF GOD

That's where a bit of biblical history is useful. As far back as the Garden of Eden when Adam and Eve first rebelled against God, a promise was made by God himself that one day the "seed" of a woman would crush the head of the serpent (the personification of the devil).[3] In other words, God was promising that one day a child would be born who would destroy the dominion and work of the evil one in our world.

This promise was later passed on to Abraham when God pledged, "All peoples on earth will be blessed through you."[4] The blessing was to come through Abraham's son Isaac. When Isaac's son Jacob was just a young man, God appeared to him in a dream and said, "All peoples on earth will be blessed through you and your offspring."[5] Later, Judah was born to Jacob and Leah.

Near the end of his life Jacob gathered all of his sons to his bedside and pronounced a blessing on them. When Judah knelt beside his elderly father, Jacob said, "You are a lion's cub, O Judah;...The scepter will not depart from Judah, nor the ruler's staff from between his feet, until he comes to whom it belongs, and the obedience of the nations is his."[6] Jacob was predicting that the royal leadership of the nation of Israel would be established through his son Judah, and God's promises to Abraham, Isaac, and Jacob would be fulfilled in him.

If we fast-forward the tape several hundred years, we discover that a young shepherd boy named David, a descendant of Jacob and Leah, was eventually chosen to be king over the entire nation. "Then the men of Judah came to Hebron and there they anointed David king over the house of *Judah*."[7] David, the greatest king in the history of Israel, a man who conquered giants, drove out foreign enemies, and established the nation as the greatest of its time, was the direct descendant of Jacob—and Leah.

Where is all this genealogy leading? And what does this have to do with Leah's faith in God?

Jump ahead to approximately 4 B.C., to a small village named Nazareth. The gospel of Luke tells us:

> In the sixth month, God sent the angel Gabriel to Nazareth, a town in Galilee, to a virgin pledged to be married to a man named Joseph, a descendant of David. The virgin's name was Mary. The angel went to her and said, "Greetings, you who are highly favored! The Lord is with you."
>
> Mary was greatly troubled at his words and wondered what kind of greeting this might be. But the angel said to her, "Do not be afraid, Mary, you have found favor with God. You will be with child and give birth to a son, and you are to give him the name Jesus. He will be great and will be called the Son of the Most High. The Lord God will give him the throne of his father David, and he will reign over the *house of Jacob* forever; his kingdom will never end."[9]

Luke puts the final piece of the puzzle in place when he gives us the family genealogy of Mary, the mother of Jesus. He traces her ancestry back through her father, Heli. Heli was a descendant of "David, the son of Jesse…the son of *Judah*, the *son of Jacob*, the son of Isaac, the son of Abraham…the son of Adam, the son of God."[10]

There it is—the story of God's mysterious working in Leah's life. Although she did not fully understand the role she was playing, she was being used by God to complete a promise made to Adam, affirmed to Abraham, and then passed on to Jacob, and from Jacob to Judah. Through Jacob and Leah's fourth son, Judah, came David, Solomon, Joseph, Mary, and eventually Jesus, the Christ. Even though Jacob may have loved Rachel more, it was through Leah that God created the ancestral line that eventually gave us the Savior.

What if Leah had simply given up on her marriage? What if she had allowed her feelings to dictate that she should leave Jacob or take another lover? God literally used Leah's faith in his higher and hidden purposes for her marriage to help accomplish the salvation of the world.

Back to the question we asked earlier: Was Leah right to believe that God was working in her life, even in her difficult relationship with Jacob? From a human standpoint the marriage was initially a disaster. It was launched in deceit and characterized by neglect. Yet from it came the most significant human being ever to walk the face of the earth, Jesus of Nazareth.

Is it an overstatement to say that because Jacob and Leah stayed in their marriage, troubled as it was, the course of human history was changed? Is it going too far to say that because Leah trusted that God was at work in her life and acknowledged his presence year after year, she became part of a plan that has shaken the world?

Let me say again, God has a higher and unseen purpose in our relationships than we can imagine. If we look at our husband or wife from a purely human standpoint, we can easily conclude it's pointless. And if it's a big mistake, why try to hang in there any longer? Why not fold our cards and leave the table? How many nights do we need to cry ourselves to sleep, or fight back tears at the dinner table, before admitting the marriage was a blunder and it's time to get out?

Let me suggest that maybe, just maybe, God has a bigger picture in mind for your life and marriage than you ever dreamed possible. But with few exceptions, that purpose won't be accomplished by choosing to give up and get out.

THE LESSONS OF JACOB AND LEAH'S STORY

What's remarkable about Leah is that she named Judah "Praise" when she had little or no idea how history was going to play itself out. But she knew there was a God in heaven who saw her suffering and misery in marriage. And rather than cashing in her relationship, she chose to go against her feelings and her circumstances and trust God instead. Despite her pain, she found it in her soul to praise him. And through her life we can draw several encouraging principles that apply to our marriages as well.

God Is Bigger Than Our Bad Decisions

For the sake of discussion, let's assume you married someone that you now wish you had not married. Your marriage is strained, your spouse is distant, and your prospects for the future are looking grim. Are your life and marriage destined for nothing but unhappiness?

That's essentially a fatalist point of view. But fatalism is based on ancient pagan philosophy, not the teaching of Scripture. In fact, the Bible knows nothing of fatalism. The Scriptures hold out the hope that with God "all things are possible."[11] Over and over again the New Testament refers to God as "the God of all hope."[12]

The truth is, God's purposes are greater than our poor choices. He can accomplish things in our lives we never imagined, in spite of our mistakes. God can use imperfect people to accomplish his perfect will.

Go back to the family tree of Jesus as an example. The ancestry of Joseph and Mary reads in some cases like a soap opera. In the list of names you will discover adulterers, prostitutes, idol worshipers, and murderers.

Why would God print such embarrassing information about the family ancestry of Joseph and Mary? After all, this is the Bible. You would think God would have edited it more carefully. But those names are there deliberately to make the point that God specializes in using damaged goods to accomplish his purposes. The doctrine of grace teaches that God shows us his mercy and favor even when we've messed up or made some major bad choices. Our one bad choice is not the final word.

God Can Pick Us Up Right Where We Are

Perhaps you did marry someone over the objections or warnings of family or friends. Perhaps you did get sexually involved too soon and now regret it. Or maybe you married someone because of your own insecurities, not because it was a good choice.

God knew you would do that even before you did. But even your bad decision is not beyond the scope of his power to take a wrong choice and use it for his purposes.

When I was in seminary, I met a pilot who had lived most of his early adult life in complete rebellion against God. His father had been a minister, but when he died of a heart attack at a young age, the son became bitter and blamed God for taking his father from him. He was out to prove he didn't need that type of God.

After college he entered the air force. Both his lifestyle and goals made it clear he would do whatever he pleased with his life. That included the choice of a wife. She was a beautiful and gentle person, but she too had chosen to live as if God didn't exist.

He survived over two hundred combat missions in North Vietnam, narrowly escaping death several times. But his rebellion had exacted a high toll on his life. One Christmas Day sitting on the runway waiting to take off on another bombing mission, he suddenly thought, What unfortunate series of decisions did I make that have put me in a place like this on Christmas?

When he returned home, he and his wife underwent an amazing transformation. He discovered that the God he had attempted to run from had refused to let him get away. And he did something he thought he would never do again, not since the day his father died. He prayed and asked God to forgive him for living as a prodigal. He decided to trust Christ for his salvation and asked God to allow him a fresh start.

Once he completed his final tour of duty, he retired and entered seminary. For many years now he and his sweet wife have been used to encourage countless people as they've ministered in several churches throughout the Southeastern United States.

Was their getting married a mistake? They never consulted God or gave much thought to how things might turn out. Yet the Heavenly Father, who can see the end from the beginning, had a plan in mind for their lives.

Nothing about Your Life Is an Accident

God has a plan in mind for you as well. There is a purpose behind your existence and a reason for your being on earth at this time. Nothing about you is accidental. Nor is your marriage too big a problem for God to solve. It didn't catch him by surprise, nor has it foiled his plans for you to serve him.

How can I be so sure? Well, can you imagine God pacing up and down the corridors of heaven, wringing his hands, muttering to himself, "What in the world am I going to do about Jim and Marcia's marriage? This one's tougher than I can handle"? I can't.

If both of you are willing to take that leap of faith and believe that God is bigger than your doubts and current problems, you may begin to discover the higher and hidden purposes in your marriage. What you'll find is that he has been working in your life far longer than you ever realized. What seems at one time like a huge mistake may turn out to be part of a masterful plan.

Back in the 1920s a young British scientist experimented with various sorts of bacteria. One night he left his petri dishes out on the counter. Much to his dismay he discovered green mold growing in one the next morning. Standard procedure in those days was to discard the dishes and start over. But for some reason, he chose not to throw out the dish with mold. As he begin to study it and conduct further experiments, he discovered it had some remarkable characteristics. In 1929 the young scientist reported to the world the discovery of penicillin. Hundreds of millions, if not billions, of lives have been saved by his "mistake."

God's Purposes Ultimately Prevail

Don't rush too soon into thinking your marriage is a meaningless relationship. The final chapter has not been written. You haven't seen everything God intends to do with your relationship. The Scriptures assure us, "So is my word that goes out from my mouth: It will not return to me empty, but will accomplish what I desire and achieve the purpose for which I sent it."[13]

What God has set out to do in your marriage he will accomplish. I urge you to look beyond your immediate circumstances and emotions and place your faith in the fact that God is working out something much higher and bigger than we can possibly imagine. If God could use Leah and Jacob's marriage, there's nothing to prevent him from doing the same in your life and mine.

John and Vera Mae Perkins are remarkable people. Together they have started efforts in rural Mississippi to help people help themselves through food cooperatives, health clinics, and much more. When I was in school, I spent an entire month with them in Jackson, Mississippi, restoring homes to sell to neighbors at a reasonable price. And I observed firsthand the strength of their relationship.

But their marriage wasn't always a bed of roses. When they were first married, they experienced such tremendous strife that they separated. Both had come to the conclusion that their marriage was a mistake. To make matters worse, Vera Mae discovered she was pregnant.

For over a year they lived in separate parts of the nation, and the marriage looked doomed. Finally, Vera Mae's mother scrimped together enough money to send her daughter to California to see John and "get it settled," which most likely meant divorce.

But when Vera Mae stepped off the bus with their firstborn son in her arms, John Perkins's hard heart melted. After they decided not to divorce, God began working in their hearts. John had a dramatic spiritual experience that changed the course of their lives. They both experienced God's call to help others. Eventually that meant going back to Mississippi to try to alleviate the suffering of impoverished people.

They paid a high price for their concern. Once John was arrested by the highway patrol, taken to a local jail, and beaten within an inch of his life. Only his wife's brave efforts demanding his release saved him.

Now John and Vera Mae work in the riot-torn neighborhoods of Los Angeles, trying to help broken families and a fractured culture. What a terrible shame if their marriage had come to a premature end forty years ago. So many people who needed their love and encouragement would have missed out. So much good would have gone undone. But God had a higher purpose for their lives than just "getting it settled." Today they serve as role models in their community, living witnesses of the fact that a "big mistake" can be transformed into a tremendous source of happiness and fulfillment.[14]

Conclusion

Are you ready to give up because you believe your marriage should never have been? The next time you attend a Christmas program with its stirring music and glorious message of a Savior born to the world, just remember that, in part, you have Jacob and Leah to thank. Leah didn't give up. She didn't choose the easy way out. She trusted that God knew what he was doing, and the world is still experiencing the results of her faith.

It may not be clear to you tomorrow, or even the next day, just what God is doing in your marriage. But if you choose to live by faith, rather than by circumstances or emotions, God will honor you and eventually give you a glimpse of his higher and hidden purposes. There's no telling what you may discover.

Chapter Ten

PLAYING FOR
KEEPS

S everal of us were playing volleyball outside one Saturday
afternoon when we were interrupted by the noise of a
wedding entourage. Horns were blaring, streamers were
flying, and wedding attendants were waving at us as they cruised
by in shining white limousines.

"You poor fool," the man next to me muttered, unaware
that anyone was listening. "You have no idea what you're getting
yourself into."

I gathered that his marriage had been less than satisfying.

If a couple doesn't get along well, or constantly feels dissatis-
fied, or frequently questions if they even love each other, can they
start over? Is there a way to replace anger and unhappiness with
love and intimacy? Yes, I believe there is a way back. It's found in
what I call the Jacob and Leah Principle of Marriage. That principle simply states: Despite a bad start, God can bless your life
together and give you a genuine love for each other.

"Wait a minute," you may be saying. "What evidence is
there that Jacob and Leah ever developed a meaningful relationship?"

I'm glad you asked. Genesis tells us that Jacob eventually decided to leave his crooked father-in-law's business. When he asked Leah and Rachel if they were willing to go with him, they both replied, "Do we still have any share in the inheritance of our father's estate?…So do whatever God has told you."[1] Despite all the hurt in Leah's life, when the moment arrived, she chose to cast her lot with her husband and leave her father behind.

After Jacob arrived in the land of Canaan, his wife Rachel died while giving birth to their second son, Benjamin. It was a devastating loss for Jacob, and he set up a pillar as a perpetual memorial over her grave. Apparently Leah outlived her sister by several more years.

Although Genesis is silent about the intervening time, we are told that decades later a famine forced Jacob to move his family to Egypt to avoid starvation. As he reached the end of his life years later, he gathered his sons around him and made one final request. He did not want to be buried in Egypt, so he tells them: "I am about to be gathered to my people. Bury me with my fathers in the cave in the field of Ephron the Hittite, the cave in the field of Machpelah, near Mamre in Canaan, which Abraham [his grandfather] bought as a burial place from Ephron the Hittite, along with the field. There Abraham and his wife Sarah were buried, there Isaac and his wife Rebekah were buried, and *there I buried Leah.*"[2] The Scriptures then tell us, "When Jacob had finished giving instructions to his sons, he drew his feet up into the bed, breathed his last and was gathered to his people."[3]

I want the full significance of this story to sink into your soul. Jacob with his final breath asks his sons to bury him—next to Leah, not Rachel. In a culture that highly regarded the sanctity of tradition and family, Jacob reminded his sons that his grandparents were buried together, his parents were buried together, and that he now wished to be buried next to his wife Leah. The very fact he buried her in the ancestral plot and asked to be placed next to her is a profound statement of his honor and esteem for her at the end of his life. The fact he regarded Leah as belonging in the same category as his grandmother and mother suggests a deeper level of intimacy, bonding, and love for Leah that had finally taken root in his heart. Although he spent the majority of his life favoring Rachel and spurning Leah, in his final years he came to see his marriage to Leah as the legacy God had blessed. He accorded her the same honor given to Sarah and Rebekah, the beloved wives of Abraham and Isaac.

That's what I mean when I say God can change your mind about the person you married.

LEARNING TO TRUST THE HEART OF GOD

Things that begin all wrong don't have to end that way. Marriage is not a straight-line graph. It may take some unexpected curves, but God can use them to bless your life together and give you a genuine love for one another. It was slow in coming, but sometime during Jacob's final years he saw that what began as a deception was actually no mistake at all. And, as history so dramatically records, his marriage to Leah was part of a glorious plan that produced David, Solomon, Joseph, Mary, and finally Jesus the Christ.

If God can heal a marriage such as Jacob and Leah's, why can't he do the same thing in your life? Why can't God take a heart of stone and replace it with a heart of tenderness toward your mate? Why can't he demonstrate to you that his plan for your life is much bigger and more magnificent than you have ever imagined? Why can't he reveal to you that's he's been operating in your life long before you ever realized it?

That's why I say there's hope for marriages that begin all

wrong or get way offtrack. Because there actually is. That hope is found in trusting God, who has revealed himself in Jesus Christ. The grace of God is available to every marriage because of the finished work of Christ on the cross. There, bearing our sins, he opened the way to a relationship with God that can literally transform our lives. As we recognize our need for forgiveness and reconciliation with God, the gift of grace is offered to us.

As the Apostle Paul once wrote, "For the wages of sin is death, but the gift of God is eternal life in Christ Jesus our Lord."[4] We don't have to attend a seminar, buy a cassette tape series, or make an exotic pilgrimage to discover this healing grace. We simply have to trust God for it.

The result is a new ability to love other people, particularly our husbands and wives. The Apostle John, often known as the Apostle of Love, wrote: "Dear friends, let us love one another, for love comes from God....This is love: not that we loved God, but that he loved us and sent his Son as an atoning sacrifice for our sins. Dear friends, since God so loved us, we also ought to love one another."[5]

The most effective way to ensure our marriage is for keeps is to turn to God. Through Jesus Christ he can give us a new love for our husband or wife. A fresh start in our relationship begins with a fresh start with God.

I read once of a couple who could never agree whether to listen to the news or classical music. After the wife began trusting in Christ's love, she surprised her husband one day by switching the channel to the news.

"Why did you do that?" he asked.

"Because I know it's what you like to listen to," she replied.

He got up and turned it back to music. From that point on the acrimony and fighting in their marriage dissipated. Why? Because the love of God allowed them to go beyond themselves to show love to the other person.

FOUR STEPS TO A FRESH START

Couples who want a fresh start in their marriage must make five important decisions.

1. Make a conscious decision before God to remain married to this person for the rest of your life.

Until we settle that issue once and for all, we will never experience a genuine fresh start. As long as we're still weighing our options, we'll never come home to our spouse. Our heart will always be elsewhere.

People in troubled relationships often fantasize to escape the difficult realities of their marriage. They see an attractive person and think, I know I'd be happy with him (or her). They refuse to invest the needed time and energy in their marriage because their thoughts are always with someone else.

Only when we stop such emotional window-shopping and decide to enjoy the purchase we made on our wedding day will our feelings begin to change. We need to say to ourselves, If I'm to enjoy Venus for a wife, or Adonis for a husband, it will have to be the person I'm married to.

Cheryl and I attended a school banquet one evening where one of the men at the head table was flirting with a woman much younger than he was. He didn't realize that anyone else noticed, but he virtually ignored his wife and spent the entire night talking to and smiling at the other woman. Unless we are firmly committed to remaining married to our mate, we will become prisoners of perpetual distraction and may embarrass ourselves in front of others.

The good news is that human beings have an amazing ability to adapt. If we decide to be contented with the person we married, we will eventually feel that contentment.

For several years I drove a car that my wife and I called our "After-dinner Mint." It earned that name because the manufacturer painted it a yellow-green combination, the colors found in the chocolate mint wafers you buy at the cash register.

It ran well, needed few major repairs, and at five hundred dollars was a steal. But the color was such an embarrassment that our son in junior high refused to let us pick him up at school in it.

Around town I received a number of dirty looks from other drivers, implying everything from, "I suppose you wear matching polyester pants," to "You know the EPA has outlawed cars like yours." My self-esteem took a number of hits as I cruised around Chicago in my yellow-green car.

But when I sat down and added up the cost of buying another car complete with tax, title, insurance, and stickers, the After-Dinner Mint always looked much better to me. When I finally sold it, it was an emotional moment for all of us.

Obviously relationships are a much more serious matter than used cars. And learning to be content with another person is a much more complex task than getting used to an old automobile. But it is true that once we decide to be satisfied with what we have, we can find a spirit of delight. To renew a marriage, both individuals need to say before God, "I choose this day to remain married to this person for the rest of my life and will not even consider any other alternative."

2. Choose to make your marriage the most important relationship in your life.

That means putting your husband or wife above your relationship with your relatives, parents, co-workers, and even children. Our order of priorities must be God first, our spouse second, our children third, and then others.

A friend in the military once told me that when he would return from active duty overseas he would first meet his wife for a day alone, leaving the children with a baby-sitter. Then he would come home and greet his children. That's the kind of priority we need to give our husbands or wives. Our relationship with our spouse needs to take precedence over time spent on the phone with our friends and relatives, rounds of golf played with clients, and commitments to worthwhile causes.

Chuck Swindoll once commented that he's attended more than one funeral where the husband wept on his shoulder and said, "I never knew what I really had until she was gone." Don't let that happen in your life. Don't wait until it's too late to make your marriage the priority it needs to be.

How do you do that? How do people act toward the most important person in their life? They talk about that person frequently, think about him or her when they're away, and say no to other people just so they can spend time together. Choosing to make our marriage our top priority relationship may seem awkward at first. The emotional satisfaction may not be strong right away. But the more time and attention both partners invest in the relationship, the more that will change.

Have you ever noticed the difference in your sexual attraction to each other when you're away alone together for an unhurried evening versus when you're cooking supper at 5:00 o'clock on a Tuesday night? For romance and courtship to flourish, you need to recreate the conditions of your dating years—time alone, time to talk, time to laugh. Couples working split shifts, two jobs, or weekends aren't giving their relationship a chance. It may call for a drastic change in your standard of living or a new budget, but if the marriage is going to survive, you have to see each other for at least fifteen hours a week.

It may also mean telling your relatives that your husband or wife comes first. Many well-meaning in-laws simply assume they have the same priority in their children's lives they once did. It can't work that way. Holidays, discretionary time, and vacations need to be considered first with our spouse's needs in mind. Both of you may agree that time should be spent with relatives, but your marriage comes first.

We also need to see our children in proper perspective. We are given them for only a few years. If our marriage has been made a top priority throughout those years, it will not only sustain us during the empty nest, it may thrive. But the time to be building that marriage is now, not when our last child graduates from high school.

Finally, we can't allow careers to disrupt our marriage. We need to remember that we work to live; we ought not live to work. Individuals who spend their entire lives giving their best shot to the company often make a sad discovery. They've reached the top of the corporate ladder, but they have left their family behind. A successful businessman once confessed he was not interested in participating in a heart disease reduction program at work. "Why would I want to live longer?" he said. "I have only a banking relationship with my family."

Choosing to make our marriage our first priority may be difficult. But we can get a fresh start only if we choose to truly "leave" all other relationships, to truly become "one" with our husband or wife.

3. Choose to act out love toward the other person.

I once heard a family seminar speaker make the profound statement, "Love is action." He was right. Essentially love is how we act toward other people.

We have several all-talk radio stations in Chicago. Twenty-four hours a day you can switch them on, and all you hear is talk. Seven days a week. Twelve months a year. Nothing but talk. It's far too easy for us as husbands or wives to be "all-talk radio" when it comes to loving our spouse. Love is not what we say, or what we intend, but what we actually do.

A few years ago we bought some canned vegetables at a giant warehouse. My wife was fixing supper a few nights later when I heard her scream.

"What's wrong?" I asked, running into the kitchen.

"That's what's wrong," she said, pointing at the pan of vegetables on the stove. Right in the middle was a mouse—a dead mouse.

There are moments in a marriage when love has to go beyond talking to doing. Doing in this case meant carrying the pan and the mummified mouse outside and disposing of it. We both hesitated. This was no ordinary dirty job; this was a major league gross-out. I won't tell you who finally did the deed, but let's just say love can sometimes be costly.

There's no substitute for doing something that's loving. What's the alternative? To stay distant, to demand the other person make the first gesture, to spend our life in loneliness and isolation just to make a point?

Love is doing for the other person all the things our selfish human nature doesn't want to do. It's leaving the last slice of pizza for someone else, spending time with their friends, and picking up the other person's dry cleaning on our way home from work. It's all the small ways we can say, "I love you more than I love me."

A Hollywood celebrity once claimed that the most important person in life ought to be ourselves. Ultimately, she said, we spend all day with ourselves, we eat with ourselves, we go to bed with ourselves. Her remarks fit the narcissistic spirit of the age, but they are pathetically misinformed. If the most important person in our lives is ourselves, we will never know true love or intimacy. Only in giving our lives away do we discover the secret of living and loving. Someone illustrated the difference between heaven and hell by saying that heaven is a place where people are eager to serve, while everyone waits to be served in hell.

If we can put aside the cult of self that has become enthroned in the last thirty years and ask what it really means to love another person, we'll discover it is doing the hard thing. It's giving up our wants, our wishes, our personal goals in favor of blessing the life of another person.

4. Choose to believe that God has an extraordinary plan for your marriage.

I want to close this book by emphasizing that nothing ever catches God by surprise. No event in our lives, no trauma, no heartache, no disappointment escapes his notice or catches him off guard. He is not the author of sin and suffering, but he is the Master of all things. That's why he has the ability to take the worst moments of our lives and give them meaning.

If anyone should know the truth of that statement, it is my friend and co-worker Marshall Shelley. Marshall and his wife, Susan, recently lost two children within three months. The first was a boy, Toby, who died two minutes after birth due to congenital birth defects. A few months later, their two-year-old daughter, Mandy, who had been born with a brain condition that left her sightless, speechless, and deaf, died of pneumonia.

But before Mandy died, she had made a powerful impression on others. A hospital employee walked into Mandy's room and said to Marshall and his wife, "I've known for some time that I've needed to get God into my life, but it never seemed to be the right time or place. I'd like you to help me get God into my life, because every time I walk by her room, I see angels hovering over her crib."

A family in Marshall's church told them that their young son had always refused to pray until he heard Mandy was sick. That night he prayed his first prayer.

A hospital volunteer, supposedly sent to comfort the family, ended up pouring out the story of her divorce, remarriage, and alienation from God. In Mandy's presence, she felt like God was real to her again.

A man in their congregation wrote the Shelleys after Mandy's death, saying, "I never held Mandy, though I occasionally stroked her cheek while my wife held her. But I learned a lot from her. You've probably seen me standing by myself against the wall in the church lobby. I don't talk to many people. I feel like an empty well. I don't have much to say. But if God can use someone like Mandy, maybe he can use an empty well like me."

Marshall and Susan have come to believe that God can take our most painful situations and transform them into something precious and meaningful. "Could a sightless, wordless, helpless infant ever be a 'successful human being'? If success is fulfilling God's purposes, I consider Mandy wildly successful."[6]

If God can accomplish his purposes in Mandy's life, can he not do the same in your life and mine? He is willing to take us just as we are, with all our weaknesses and problems, and accomplish some magnificent purpose for our lives and marriage.

PLAY FOR KEEPS

I never met my grandmother, Eva Moeller. She died on the dusty and lonely plains of a western prairie state when my father was just seventeen years old. Yet my father credits her with pointing him toward God at an early age. So profound was her impact on his life that at her graveside he vowed never to do anything that would dishonor her memory.

Apart from that, I knew little about her until a few summers ago when I attended a large family reunion in the Midwest. Sitting across the table from me was one of my father's relatives. I decided to ask her about my grandmother, now gone for over fifty years.

She looked a bit nervous and then said, "Don't tell anyone I told you this."

Now I was more than a little curious. "Certainly, what is it?"

"As far as we know, your grandmother was a mail-order bride. Your grandfather was a bachelor, homesteading on the prairie where there were very few women. We believe she must have answered an advertisement to come west."

When I later relayed the information to my sisters, they filled in a part of the story I had never heard. As my grandfather was dying, he asked everyone to leave the room except my two oldest sisters. He was then eighty-nine and had been a widower for nearly thirty years.

"Do you know why I never remarried?" he asked in a raspy voice.

The two young girls shook their heads no.

"Because when your grandmother died, I realized I could never love another woman as much as I loved her."

I tell this story to make a point. If indeed my grandfather and grandmother began their marriage through a mail-order arrangement and yet learned to love each other that deeply, who's to say God can't do something just as extraordinary in your marriage?

If, like Jacob and Leah, you started out all wrong, who's to say God can't use your relationship to bless not only your lives but future generations as well?

Who's to say your marriage hasn't been in the plan of God from eternity past?

Why not begin your fresh start today? All of heaven is on

your side. Christ himself wants you to succeed. You have nothing to lose but your unhappiness.

Take the chance to start all over again. And may the God of all hope be with you both.

Chapter One: Is Love Only for the Lucky or the Strong?

1. Lawrence Kurdek, "The Relations between Well-being and Divorce History, Availability of a Proximate Adult, and Gender," *Journal of Marriage and the Family* 53 (February 1991): 71-78. See also Alan Booth and John Edwards, "Starting Over: Why Remarriages Are More Stable," *Journal of Family Issues* 13 (June 1992): 179-94.

Chapter Two: Checking In at Heartbreak Hotel

1. Genesis 29:21-27.
2. Ibid., 30.
3. Ibid., 32.
4. Ibid., 33.
5. Ibid., 34.
6. Proverbs 31:30.
7. Anastasia Toufexis, "The Right Chemistry," *Time* 141, no. 7 (February 15, 1993): 49-51.
8. Alfred DeMaris and Vaninadha Rao, "Premarital Cohabitation and Subsequent Marital Stability in the United States: A Reassessment," *Journal of Marriage and the Family* 54, no. 1 (February 1992): 178-90.
9. Frank Furstenberg, "Bringing Back the Shotgun Wedding," *Public Interest* 90 (Winter 1988): 121-27.

Chapter Three: Searching for the Escape Clause

1. Arland Thorton, "Changing Attitudes toward Family Issues in the United States," *Journal of Marriage and the Family* 51 (November 1989): 873-93.
2. Matthew 19:3-6.
3. Leslie Morgan, "Economic Well-being Following Marital Termination: A Comparison of Widowed and Divorced Women," *Journal of Family Issues* 10 (March 1989): 86-101.
4. "Breaking the Divorce Cycle," *Newsweek* (January 13, 1992): 48.
5. Ibid., 49.
6. Ibid.
7. Proverbs 5:15-17.
8. Ibid., 6:27-29.

9. Ibid., 32-33.

10. Gregory Smith et al., "Predicting Relationship Satisfaction from Couples' Use of Leisure Time," *American Journal of Family Therapy* 16, no. 1 (Spring 1988): 3-13.

11. Bob Moeller, "When Your Children Pay the Price," *Leadership Journal* 14, no. 2 (Spring 1993): 86-95.

12. Proverbs 5:18-19.

13. William Willimon, "Risky Business," *Christianity Today* (February 19, 1988): 24-25.

14. Elizabeth Thomas and Ugo Collela, "Cohabitation and Marital Stability: Quality or Commitment," *Journal of Marriage and the Family* 54, no. 2 (May 1992): 759-67.

15. Willimon, "Risky Business," 24.

16. Robert Lauer et al., "The Long-term Marriage: Perceptions of Stability and Satisfaction," *International Journal of Aging and Human Development* 31, no. 3 (1990): 189-95.

Chapter Four: If You Keep Your Vows, They'll Keep You

1. Lesley Dormen, "The Five Turning Points of Love," *Glamour* (February 1992): 192.

2. Ibid., 192-193.

3. Matthew 19:4-7.

4. "My Problem: I Was Still in Love with My Ex-husband," *Good Housekeeping* (July 1991): 26-27.

5. Matthew 22:37-39.

6. 1 Corinthians 13:4-7.

7. Quoted in "Secrets of Staying Together," *Reader's Digest* (March 1989): 152.

8. Ibid., 154.

9. Ecclesiastes 2:10-11.

Chapter 5: Investing in the Bonding Market

1. Donald Joy, Ph.D., *Re-bonding: Preventing and Restoring Damaged Relationships* (Waco: Word, 1986), 5.

2. Ibid., 10-11.

3. Ibid., 19.

4. Ibid.

5. Donald Joy, *Bonding: Relationships in the Image of God* (Waco: Word, 1985), 51.

Chapter 6: Can We Talk?

1. Lois Leiderman Davitz, Ph.D., "Why Men Divorce," *McCall's* (March 1987): 26.
2. Ibid., 26, 30.
3. Ibid., 30.
4. Ibid.
5. Norman Shawchuck, *How to Manage Conflict in the Church: Understanding and Managing Conflict*. 2 vols. (Indianapolis: Spiritual Growth Resources, 1983), 23-25, and Kenneth Thomas, *The Handbook of Industrial and Organizational Psychology*, vol. 2.
6. Shawchuck, ibid., 46-47.
7. Janet Long Harris, "What If I Married the Wrong Person?" *Today's Christian Woman* (September/October 1992): 61.
8. Shawchuck, *Manage Conflict*, 46-47.
9. Scott Winokur, "What Happy Couples Do Right," *Redbook* (June 1991): 66.
10. Ibid.
11. Shawchuck, *Manage Conflict*, 47.
12. Winokur, *Happy Couples*, 66.
13. Ibid., 66-67.
14. Ibid.
15. Shawchuck, *Manage Conflict*, 36.
16. Shawchuck, *Manage Conflict*, 37.
17. Ibid.
18. Lynne Hybels, "I Was Fit to Be Tied," *Today's Christian Woman* 13, no. 6 (November/December 1991): 82-83.

Chapter Seven: Making War, Not Love

1. Norval Glenn and Charles Weaver, "The Changing Relationship of Marital Status to Reported Happiness," *Journal of Marriage and the Family* 50, no. 7 (May 1988): 317-24.
2. 1 Corinthians 7.3-5.
3. Bill Hybels, *Honest to God: Becoming an Authentic Christian* (Grand Rapids, Mich.: Zondervan, 1990), 56-58.
4. Ibid.
5. Dave Wilkinson, "To Illustrate," *Leadership Journal* 5, no. 2 (Spring 1984): 44.

Chapter 8: Three True Aphrodisiacs

1. Genesis 30:14-16.
2. Dolf Zillman and Jennings Bryant, "Effect of Prolonged Consumption of Pornography on Family Values," *Journal of Family Issues* 9, no. 4 (December 1988): 518-44.
3. "The War Within," *Leadership Journal* 8, no. 4 (Fall 1992): 97-112.
4. 1 Corinthians 7:4.

Chapter Nine: Was It All a Mistake?

1. Genesis 29:32-33; 30:17, 19-20 (italics added by author).
2. Ibid., 29:35.
3. Ibid., 3:15.
4. Ibid., 12:3.
5. Ibid., 28:14.
6. Ibid., 49:1-10.
7. 2 Samuel 2:4 (italics added by author).
8. Micah 5:2 (italics added by author).
9. Luke 1:26-33 (italics added by author).
10. Ibid., 3:23-38 (italics added by author).
11. Matthew 19:26.
12. Romans 15:13.
13. Isaiah 55:11.
14. Vera Mae Perkins, "How I Stayed Married for 40 Years," *Urban Family* pt. 1, 1, no. 3 (Fall 1992): 28-29.

Chapter Ten: Playing for Keeps

1. Genesis 31:14.
2. Ibid., 49:29-32 (italics added by author).
3. Ibid., 33.
4. Romans 6:23.
5. 1 John 4:7, 10.
6. Marshall Shelley, "The Sightless, Wordless Theologian," *Christianity Today* 37, no. 5 (April 26, 1993): 34-36.